Cable Knit Style

15 Stunning Patterns for Pullovers, Cardigans, Tanks, Tees & More

Joan Ho
Creator of
Knitwear by Joan

PAGE STREET
PUBLISHING CO.

PAGE STREET
PUBLISHING CO.

First published in 2023 by
Page Street Publishing Co.
27 Congress Street, Suite 1511
Salem, MA 01970
www.pagestreetpublishing.com

Distributed by Macmillan, sales in Canada by The Canadian Manda Group.

27   26   25   24   23   1   2   3   4   5

ISBN-13: 978-1-64567-836-6
ISBN-10: 1-64567-836-9

Library of Congress Control Number: 2022950262

Cover and book design by Vienna Gambol for Page Street Publishing Co.
Photography by Jacky Lam

Printed and bound in the United States of America

TO ALL THE MAKERS
May the spark that lights our inspiration never fade.

CONTENTS

Introduction

Growing up, I always had an interest in fashion. Whether I was mindlessly doodling in my sketchbook or cutting up and "repurposing" my clothes into brand-new outfits (sorry Mom), I have always had a fascination with making pretty things to wear. I was first introduced to knitting back in high school, but my finished projects were limited to misshapen scarves, phone cozies and the occasional hat that I would start but never finish. Frustrated by the lack of guidance and instructions available to me, my confidence fell and I pursued other hobbies.

Fast forward a decade. Feeling bored in my spare time, I revisited my long-lost hobby. With the growing popularity of YouTube, Instagram and Pinterest, however, there was no lack of inspiration this time around. In fact, what I found was a budding community of like-minded individuals who loved sharing their projects and ideas just as much as they enjoyed making them. Social media made it possible for me to meet other makers who share a passion for fiber arts and beyond. For the first time, I was able to build connections with makers from all over the globe: Knitting was our common language.

It was then that I discovered the magical world of knitting patterns in the form of books, magazines and video tutorials. Rather than the trial-and-error (mostly error) technique from my high school years, I could finally follow a set of instructions and recreate something functional and beautiful to wear. Gone were the days of a seemingly endless number of infinity scarves, clothes for phones and ill-fitting hats.

As I gained more experience and fell more deeply in love with the craft, I delved into pattern writing. I saw it as an extension and reflection of my personal style. Whenever I couldn't find a pattern for something, I'd try my hand at making it up from scratch. I found myself once again doodling in sketchbooks, but this time with intention and purpose. My new goal was to create beautiful garments and accessories with precise attention to detail. My designs can be described as modern and functional with a store-bought quality. I never shy away from pushing the boundaries of design and incorporating other crafts, notions and hardware into my patterns. I am a big fan of texture, and one of the best ways to achieve this is through cable knitting.

Cable knitting can seem quite daunting. And while it's not the most mindless type of knitting, the techniques involved are logical, fun and rewarding. Cables are a dynamic way to bring three-dimensional details to an otherwise simple knitting project. In this pattern book, I explore a wide array of cable-knit sweaters and tops. I had the time of my life playing with different yarn weights, swatches and stitch combinations. There are designs that feature complex panels of cables, and there are designs with simpler repetitions. Cables can be at the forefront or combined with another design element to take a background role. The designs can be paired with a chunky yarn to create a bold statement piece, or a lightweight yarn for a dainty, graceful sensibility. Regardless, each piece has its own unique flair and was designed with both elegance and comfort in mind.

My inspiration for this book can be found on the concrete runway, otherwise known as the streets. I am obsessed with streetstyle fashion, the diverse and unique ensembles I've seen on my travels abroad and the effortless ways in which they're worn. With that vision in mind, I wanted to create a collection of cabled garments with an urban influence, while also maintaining a hint of tradition. The patterns are feminine and chic, but not overly trendy so they can still be appreciated for years to come.

My biggest hope for this project is to guide and inspire you, just as other designers have done and continue to do for me. All the patterns in this book are size-inclusive, ranging from XS to 6XL. One size cannot possibly fit all, and there is no better expression of self-love than to create something that showcases and celebrates your individual shape.

The most rewarding aspect of my maker journey is being able to see my designs lovingly made, worn and cherished by other members of the handmade community. I can't wait to be wardrobe twins with you! Please share your finished projects by tagging #CableKnitStyle and @knitwearbyjoan. I'm so excited to see what you come up with.

Happy making!

Before You Begin

PATTERN DIFFICULTY LEVELS

Due to the cable knitting techniques used in the patterns, some knitting experience is recommended for all of the projects in this book. The patterns range from Advanced Beginner to Advanced.

The pattern difficulty level is dependent on the complexity of the cables, the construction methods chosen and the other design elements used. The cable patterns in this book are charted—the Knitting Charts section (page 10) will give an overview of how to approach them.

Advanced Beginner: Patterns classified as Advanced Beginner are a suitable choice for those new to garment making. The Morning Glory Vest (page 83) is designated as Advanced Beginner due to the simpler nature of the moss stitch and cables. The super bulky nature of the design also makes it a quick project to make.

Intermediate: Most patterns in this book fall under this level designation. These patterns typically involve more elaborate cables, shaping and other special techniques.

Advanced: This level designation is a suitable choice if you are experienced in garment making and are comfortable with incorporating more advanced finishing techniques into your projects. The Ginger Zip (page 23) is designated as Advanced due to the zipper installation which requires hand sewing skills.

EASE & SELECTING YOUR SIZE

Every pattern in this book will include a schematic along with a sizing table. A schematic is a visual rendering of a design that provides an overview of the size and shape of the piece. The schematic provides a point of reference for determining the fit of a garment. The patterns in this book are designed and graded according to the Craft Yarn Council Standard Body Measurements.

The sizing table provides specific measurements of the finished garment and will typically include the following measurements, listed in both metric and imperial equivalents:

Body circumference: measured at the widest point of the garment, typically at the bust. Please note that the full bust measurement is not the same number as your bra size. While your bra band is equivalent to your underbust measurement, the full bust is the largest part of your chest. However, you can select another size depending on your preference for ease.

Garment length: the length of the garment from the bottom of the top (usually the ribbing) to the top of the shoulders.

Armhole depth: the vertical measurement of the underarm opening to the shoulder seams.

Sleeve circumference (if applicable): measured at the top of the sleeve. This is typically the widest point of the sleeve and corresponds with the upper bicep measurement.

Sleeve length (if applicable): the length of the sleeve from the underarm to the cuffs. Note that drop-shoulder sleeves are typically shorter in length than set-in sleeves.

Understanding Ease

Ease is the way a garment fits on your body. In reference to knitwear design, there are three types of ease: positive ease, neutral (or zero) ease and negative ease. The patterns in this book will recommend the type and amount of ease to guide you in selecting the correct size. These recommendations are based on the chest circumference of both the finished garment and the wearer.

Positive ease: This means that the finished measurements of a garment are larger than the measurements of the person wearing it. The additional fabric allows the wearer to move more comfortably and freely. A classic fit has several inches of ease, while some designs suggest significantly more ease for a relaxed fit. The majority of patterns in this book are intended to be worn with positive ease.

Neutral ease: This means that the finished measurements of a garment are equal to the measurements of the person wearing it. This type of fit results in a form-fitting garment. The Magnolia Top (page 121) is intended to be worn with neutral ease.

Negative ease: This means the finished measurements of a garment are smaller than the measurements of the person wearing it. This fit allows for the knit fabric to stretch and hug your shape when you put it on. The Azalea Top (page 127) and Azalea Cardigan (page 135) are intended to be worn with negative ease.

YARN & GAUGE

While specific yarns are recommended for all the projects in this book, you can also substitute them for others. If you decide to use an alternate yarn, I recommend selecting a substitute that is as close as possible to the original in thickness, weight and texture. That way, your finished garment will have a similar appearance, drape and wearability as the original pieces depicted in this book.

YarnSub (yarnsub.com) is an excellent resource to help you find yarn substitutes. All you have to do is type in the name of the yarn used in a pattern, and the search results will return a list of substitute yarns based on gauge, texture and fiber content. Ravelry (ravelry.com/yarns) also provides a comprehensive directory of both current and discontinued yarns. I recommend calculating the amount of yarn you will need by the yards or meters rather than by weight. Always allocate enough yarn in the same dye lot to ensure there are no color variances and that your knit project is the same color throughout.

How to Knit a Gauge Swatch

A swatch is a piece of fabric, typically a square or rectangle in shape, that you knit prior to starting a pattern. The goal of swatching is to simulate the size and fit of your project as closely as possible to the original pattern. Although recommended knitting needle size(s) are provided for each pattern, every knitter has their own unique tension which will influence the swatch and, therefore, the size and fit of the finished garment.

Each pattern in this book will provide the required stitch pattern(s) to swatch. Cable stitch patterns tend to pull in and require more stitches to fill in the same space compared to uncrossed stitch patterns such as stockinette stitch. Therefore, it is crucial to swatch and block all the different stitch patterns provided. Follow the below steps to successfully prepare for knitting your project:

Knit a swatch in the specified pattern: Knit a swatch that is large enough to represent the stitch pattern on the garment. All the patterns in this book call for a gauge within a 4-inch (10-cm) square. Therefore, it is recommended to knit at least a 5-inch (13-cm) square to account for any significant tension differences between your swatch and the one listed in the book.

The swatch pattern will specify whether it should be worked flat or in the round. Circular knitting can produce a different gauge than flat knitting due to a subtle variation in tension between knitting and purling. As such, it is important to knit your swatch as noted in the pattern for the best results.

Block the swatch: Block your swatch in the same manner you will use when finishing the final project. My preferred blocking method of choice is wet blocking, but your mileage may vary. You may notice the effects of blocking vary from yarn to yarn significantly.

Measure the swatch: Lay your swatch on a flat surface. Using a stitch gauge or simply a ruler, count and note the number of stitches within 4 inches (10 cm). Afterwards, count and note the number of rows/rounds within 4 inches (10 cm).

Make adjustments if necessary: Compare your gauge to the pattern and make adjustments if necessary. If you count more stitches per inch/cm on your swatch than is required for pattern gauge, you will need to swatch again with a larger needle. If no adjustments are made, your finished garment will be smaller than the measurements listed in the pattern.

If there are fewer stitches per inch/cm, you will need to use a smaller needle to achieve the correct gauge. If no adjustments are made, your finished garment will be larger than the measurements listed in the pattern.

If neither scenario occurs and your gauge matches, congratulations! You are ready to begin knitting your project.

KNITTING CHARTS

A knitting chart is a visual representation of knitting stitches in a pattern. Charts are most commonly used for cable, lace or colorwork knitting. Rather than through text, symbols are used to denote a specific stitch pattern. Each cell represents one (1) stitch, and each row of cells represents one (1) row or round.

Knitting charts are beneficial for multiple reasons. Charts help you visualize the design as a whole by allowing you to "preview" where the twists and turns will occur in the pattern. Knitting charts are also more efficient because there are only one set of instructions for both flat and circular knitting.

How Do You Read a Knitting Chart?

All charts are read from the bottom up. The numbers on the left and/or right side of the chart represent that row or round. Once you have reached the top of the chart, you will start over from the beginning (row/round 1).

Every chart has a legend that defines what each of the symbols means. Each pattern has an abbreviations table with further instructions on what these symbols represent.

When working flat, the chart is read from right to left on right side (RS) rows and left to right on wrong side (WS) rows.

Flat Knitting Chart

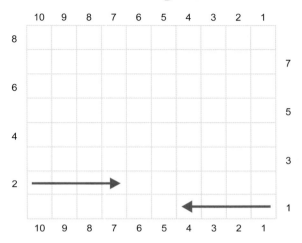

When working in the round, the cable chart is read from right to left on all rounds.

In the Round Knitting Chart

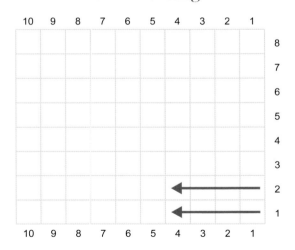

For simplicity, if a pattern calls for both knitting flat and knitting in the round, the knitting chart will have row numbering on both sides.

FASHION FORWARD

Garments for Layering & Coordinating

Cable-knit sweaters may be classic in origin, but their techniques can be adapted to trendy knitwear patterns. Contemporary knitwear is an eclectic combination of modern stitchwork in a traditional silhouette, traditional stitchwork in a modern silhouette or a mix of both, resulting in stylish and cozy pieces.

This chapter includes designs that are modern must-haves. The Ginger Zip (page 23) showcases a cabled textured pattern in a standard athletic fit. The all-around ribbing, mock neck and quarter zip fastening create a casual but distinguished urban look. The Myrtle Tee (page 33) is a modern and elevated take on the polo shirt, perfect for moments of leisure or relaxation at home. This chapter also includes two vests featuring cables and bobbles but finished with a different neckline and cut, resulting in two wholly unique garments. Both patterns have a place in any cozy wardrobe: the fuzzy Winterberry Slipover (page 15) with its high round neck and the Juniper Vest (page 45) with a V-neckline and relaxed fit. Whatever you fancy, these sweaters will run up the mileage in your rotation of outfits.

Winterberry Slipover

Known for its seasonal resilience and playful appearance, the winterberry is a species of holly native to my home province of Ontario. Much like the plant, the Winterberry Slipover is designed to be a year-round staple in any wardrobe. Whether worn on its own or layered over a blouse, the textured cables and bobbles will stand out and add a wow factor to any outfit. Knit with a strand each of worsted weight wool and mohair lace, the result is a fuzzy and plush fabric that is quick to knit and feels luxurious against the skin.

Construction Notes

The slipover is worked flat in pieces with the sides and shoulders seamed later. Stitches are picked up for both the armhole and neck edges, both of which are worked in ribbing and folded inwards for a professional finish.

SKILL LEVEL

Intermediate

SIZING

XS (S, M, L, XL) (2XL, 3XL, 4XL, 5XL, 6XL)
32.5 (36.25, 40, 44, 48.25) (52.25, 56, 60, 64.5, 68.25)″ / 82.5 (92, 101.5, 111.75, 122.5) (132.75, 142.25, 152.5, 163.75, 173.25) cm, blocked

MATERIALS

Yarn

DK weight, Phildar Phil Ecolaine in Ecru (100% Wool), 137 yds (125 m) per 50-g skein
held with
Lace weight, DROPS Brushed Alpaca Silk in Off White (77% Alpaca, 23% Silk), 153 yds (140 m) per 25-g skein

Any DK/worsted and lace weight yarn held together can be used for this pattern as long as it matches gauge. If using a single strand of yarn, any bulky weight yarn can be used as a substitute as long as it matches gauge.

Yardage/Meterage

685 (785, 900, 1040, 1120) (1255, 1390, 1520, 1585, 1665) yds / 625 (720, 825, 950, 1025) (1150, 1275, 1390, 1450, 1525) m of DK or worsted weight yarn *held with*
685 (785, 900, 1040, 1120) (1255, 1390, 1520, 1585, 1665) yds / 625 (720, 825, 950, 1025) (1150, 1275, 1390, 1450, 1525) m of textured lace weight yarn

Needles

For ribbing: US 8 (5 mm), 24- to 60-inch (60- to 150-cm) circular needles
For body: US 9 (5.5 mm), 24- to 60-inch (60- to 150-cm) circular needles
For neckline and armhole edge: US 8 (5 mm), 16- to 24-inch (40- to 60-cm) circular needles

Notions

Cable needle
Scissors
Stitch marker(s)
Tapestry needle

GAUGE

22 sts x 24 rows = 4 inches (10 cm) in 1x1 ribbing worked flat using smaller needles (blocked)

21 sts x 24 rows = 4 inches (10 cm) in Chart A worked flat using larger needles (blocked) Choose any section of the chart for your swatch.

TECHNIQUES

Horizontal Invisible Seam (page 161)
Longtail Cast On (page 157)
Vertical Invisible Seam (page 161)
Whip Stitch (page 162)

ABBREVIATIONS

0 or -	no stitch / step does not apply to your size
1x1 ribbing	*k1, p1; repeat from * until end
cn	cable needle
k	knit
k1tbl	knit through the back loop
k2tog	knit two stitches together [1 st decreased]
p	purl
p2tog	purl 2 sts together [1 st decreased]
patt	pattern
pm	place marker
rem	remain(ing)
RS	right side
sl1wyib	slip 1 st purlwise with yarn in back
sl1wyif	slip 1 st purlwise with yarn in front
st(s)	stitch(es)
work(ing) even	continue working the pattern as established without any increases or decreases
WS	wrong side
yo	yarnover

Cable stitch abbreviations can be found in the Legend on page 21.

SIZING CHART

		XS	S	M	L	XL	2XL	3XL	4XL	5XL	6XL
A) Body circumference	in	32.5	36.25	40	44	48.5	52.25	56	60	64.5	68.25
	cm	82.5	92	101.5	111.75	122.5	132.75	142.25	152.5	163.75	173.25
B) Garment length	in	19	21	22	23	24	25	26.5	27.5	28.5	30
	cm	48.25	53.25	56	58.5	61	63.5	67.25	69.75	72.5	76.25
C) Armhole depth	in	7.5	8	8.5	9	9.5	10	10.5	11	11.5	12
	cm	19	20.25	21.5	22.75	24.25	25.5	26.75	28	29.25	30.5

This sweater is designed with 2–4 inches (5–10 cm) of positive ease. Sample shown is knit in size XS.

SCHEMATIC

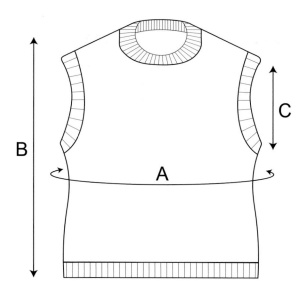

WINTERBERRY SLIPOVER PATTERN

FRONT

Using US 8 (5 mm) needles, cast on 88 (98, 108, 118, 130) (140, 150, 160, 172, 182) sts using the longtail cast on method.

Work in 1x1 ribbing for 1.5 inches (3.75 cm), ending on a WS Row.

Switch to US 9 (5.5 mm) needles.

Set-up row 1 (RS): P6 (11, 5, 10, 5) (10, 15, 9, 15, 9), work row 1 of Chart A (pages 20 and 21), p6 (11, 5, 10, 5) (10, 15, 9, 15, 9).

Set-up row 2 (WS): K6 (11, 5, 10, 5) (10, 15, 9, 15, 9), work row 2 of Chart A, k6 (11, 5, 10, 5) (10, 15, 9, 15, 9).

Continue working in patt as established until the piece measures 10.5 (12, 12.5, 13, 13.5) (14, 15, 15.5, 16, 17) inches / 26.75 (30.5, 31.75, 33, 34.25) (35.5, 38, 39.25, 40.75, 43.25) cm from the cast on edge. Your last row should be a WS row.

Bind off 3 sts at the beginning of the next 2 rows, working rem sts in patt [82 (92, 102, 112, 124) (134, 144, 154, 166, 176) sts rem].

Bind off 1 st at the beginning of the next 6 rows, working rem sts in patt [76 (86, 96, 106, 118) (128, 138, 148, 160, 170) sts rem].

Work even until the piece measures 15.5 (17.5, 18.5, 19.5, 20.5) (21.5, 23, 24, 25, 26.5) inches / 39.25 (44.5, 47, 49.5, 52) (54.5, 58.5, 61, 63.5, 67.25) cm from the cast on edge. Your last row should be a WS row. If possible, avoid ending on rows 10 or 16 of the chart.

Next row (RS): Work 32 (37, 42, 47, 52) (57, 62, 66, 72, 77) sts in patt, bind off 12 (12, 12, 12, 14) (14, 14, 16, 16, 16) sts, work rem 32 (37, 42, 47, 52) (57, 62, 66, 72, 77) sts in patt. Leave front left sts on a holder or spare yarn to return to later.

TIP: Mark where you left off in the chart.

NOTE: For cables that no longer have the full amount of sts, you can k those sts on the RS and p on the WS. In instances where only one side of a cable is reduced, continue cabling the remaining side.

FRONT RIGHT
Row 1 (WS): Work in patt.

Row 2 (RS): Bind off 1 st, work in patt until end [31 (36, 41, 46, 51) (56, 61, 65, 71, 76) sts rem].

Repeat the last 2 rows a total of 4 more times [27 (32, 37, 42, 47) (52, 57, 61, 67, 72) sts rem].

Work even until the piece measures 18 (20, 21, 22, 23) (24, 25.5, 26.5, 27.5, 29) inches / 45.75 (50.75, 53.25, 56, 58.5) (61, 64.75, 67.25, 69.75, 73.75) cm from the cast on edge. Your last row should be a RS row.

Row 1 (WS): Bind off 7 (8, 10, 11, 12) (13, 15, 16, 17, 18) sts, work in patt until end [20 (24, 27, 31, 35) (39, 42, 45, 50, 54) sts rem].
Row 2 and all RS rows: Work in patt.
Row 3: Bind off 7 (8, 10, 11, 12) (13, 15, 16, 17, 18) sts, work in patt until end [13 (16, 17, 20, 23) (26, 27, 29, 33, 36) sts rem].
Row 5: Bind off 7 (8, 9, 10, 12) (13, 14, 15, 17, 18) sts, work in patt until end [6 (8, 8, 10, 11) (13, 13, 14, 16, 18) sts rem].
Row 7: Bind off rem 6 (8, 8, 10, 11) (13, 13, 14, 16, 18) sts.

Break the yarn, leaving a tail that is double the length of the shoulder for seaming.

FRONT LEFT
Rejoin the yarn to WS of work.

Row 1 (WS): Bind off 1 st, work in patt until end.
Row 2 (RS): Work in patt [31 (36, 41, 46, 51) (56, 61, 65, 71, 76) sts rem].
Repeat the last 2 rows a total of 4 more times [27 (32, 37, 42, 47) (52, 57, 61, 67, 72) sts rem].

Work even until the piece measures 18 (20, 21, 22, 23) (24, 25.5, 26.5, 27.5, 29) inches / 45.75 (50.75, 53.25, 56, 58.5) (61, 64.75, 67.25, 69.75, 73.75) cm from the cast on edge. Your last row should be a WS row.

Row 1 (RS): Bind off 7 (8, 10, 11, 12) (13, 15, 16, 17, 18) sts, work in patt until end [20 (24, 27, 31, 35) (39, 42, 45, 50, 54) sts rem].
Row 2 and all WS rows: Work in patt.
Row 3: Bind off 7 (8, 10, 11, 12) (13, 15, 16, 17, 18) sts, work in patt until end [13 (16, 17, 20, 23) (26, 27, 29, 33, 36) sts rem].
Row 5: Bind off 7 (8, 9, 10, 12) (13, 14, 15, 17, 18) sts, work in patt until end [6 (8, 8, 10, 11) (13, 13, 14, 16, 18) sts rem].
Row 7: Bind off rem 6 (8, 8, 10, 11) (13, 13, 14, 16, 18) sts.

Break the yarn, leaving a tail that is double the length of the shoulder for seaming.

BACK
Using US 8 (5 mm) needles, cast on 88 (98, 108, 118, 130) (140, 150, 160, 172, 182) sts using the longtail cast on method.

Work in 1x1 ribbing for 1.5 inches (3.75 cm), ending on a WS row.

Switch to US 9 (5.5 mm) needles.

Set-up row 1 (RS): P6 (11, 5, 10, 5) (10, 15, 9, 15, 9), work row 1 of Chart A, p6 (11, 5, 10, 5) (10, 15, 9, 15, 9).
Set-up row 2 (WS): K6 (11, 5, 10, 5) (10, 15, 9, 15, 9), work row 2 of Chart A, k6 (11, 5, 10, 5) (10, 15, 9, 15, 9).

Continue working in patt as established until the piece measures 10.5 (12, 12.5, 13, 13.5) (14, 15, 15.5, 16, 17) inches / 26.75 (30.5, 31.75, 33, 34.25) (35.5, 38, 39.25, 40.75, 43.25) cm from the cast on edge. Your last row should be a WS row.

Bind off 3 sts at the beginning of the next 2 rows, working rem sts in patt [82 (92, 102, 112, 124) (134, 144, 154, 166, 176) sts rem].

Bind off 1 st at the beginning of the next 6 rows, working rem sts in patt [76 (86, 96, 106, 118) (128, 138, 148, 160, 170) sts rem].

Work even until the piece measures 18 (20, 21, 22, 23) (24, 25.5, 26.5, 27.5, 29) inches / 45.75 (50.75, 53.25, 56, 58.5) (61, 64.75, 67.25, 69.75, 73.75) cm from the cast on edge. Your last row should be a WS row.

Next row (RS): Bind off 7 (8, 10, 11, 12) (13, 15, 16, 17, 18) sts, work 23 (27, 30, 34, 38) (42, 45, 48, 53, 57) sts in patt, bind off 16 (16, 16, 16, 18) (18, 18, 20, 20, 20) sts, work rem 30 (35, 40, 45, 50) (55, 60, 64, 70, 75) sts in patt. Leave back right sts on a separate holder or spare yarn to return to later.

TIP: Mark where you left off in the chart.

Back Left
Row 1 (WS): Bind off 7 (8, 10, 11, 12) (13, 15, 16, 17, 18) sts, work in patt until end [23 (27, 30, 34, 38) (42, 45, 48, 53, 57) sts rem].
Row 2 (RS): Bind off 1 st at the neck edge, work in patt until end [22 (26, 29, 33, 37) (41, 44, 47, 52, 56) sts rem].
Row 3: Bind off 7 (8, 10, 11, 12) (13, 15, 16, 17, 18) sts, work in patt until end [15 (18, 19, 22, 25) (28, 29, 31, 35, 38) sts rem].
Row 4: Bind off 1 st at the neck edge, work in patt until end [14 (17, 18, 21, 24) (27, 28, 30, 34, 37) sts rem].
Row 5: Bind off 7 (8, 9, 10, 12) (13, 14, 15, 17, 18) sts, work in patt until end [7 (9, 9, 11, 12) (14, 14, 15, 17, 19) sts rem].

Row 6: Bind off 1 st at the neck edge, work in patt until end [6 (8, 8, 10, 11) (13, 13, 14, 16, 18) sts rem].
Row 7: Bind off rem 6 (8, 8, 10, 11) (13, 13, 14, 16, 18) sts and break the yarn.

Back Right
Rejoin the yarn to WS of work.
Row 1 (WS): Bind 1 off st at the neck edge, work in patt until end [22 (26, 29, 33, 37) (41, 44, 47, 52, 56) sts rem].
Row 2 (RS): Bind off 7 (8, 10, 11, 12) (13, 15, 16, 17, 18) sts, work in patt until end [15 (18, 19, 22, 25) (28, 29, 31, 35, 38) sts rem].
Row 3: Bind 1 off st at the neck edge, work in patt until end [14 (17, 18, 21, 24) (27, 28, 30, 34, 37) sts rem].
Row 4: Bind off 7 (8, 9, 10, 12) (13, 14, 15, 17, 18) sts, work in patt until end [7 (9, 9, 11, 12) (14, 14, 15, 17, 19) sts rem].
Row 5: Bind 1 off st at the neck edge, work in patt until end [6 (8, 8, 10, 11) (13, 13, 14, 16, 18) sts rem].
Row 6: Bind off rem 6 (8, 8, 10, 11) (13, 13, 14, 16, 18) sts and break the yarn.

SEAMING THE BODY
Using a tapestry needle and the same yarn, use the horizontal invisible seaming technique to seam the shoulders. Use the vertical invisible seaming technique to seam the sides, beginning with the cast on edge up until the bind off edge of the underarm.

ARMHOLE EDGE (MAKE 2)
Using US 8 (5 mm) needles and beginning with the center of the underarm, pick up and k3 from bind off edge. Evenly pick up and k34 (36, 39, 41, 44) (47, 50, 52, 55, 58) towards the shoulder, and then evenly pick up and k34 (36, 39, 41, 44) (47, 50, 52, 55, 58) towards the underarm. Pick up and k3 from the remaining bind off edge. Pm and join for working in the round [74 (78, 84, 88, 94) (100, 106, 110, 116, 122) sts].

Work in 1x1 ribbing for 3 inches (7.5 cm). Bind off loosely. Break the yarn, leaving a tail that is double the length of the armhole. Turn the bind off edge inwards and whip stitch the bind off edge to cast on edge.

NECKBAND
Using US 8 (5 mm) needles, beginning with the center of the left shoulder, pick up and k19 towards the center front, pick up and k12 (12, 12, 12, 14) (14, 14, 16, 16, 16) from the front center bind off sts, pick up and k19 towards the center of the right shoulder, pick up and k9 towards the center back, pick up and k16 (16, 16, 16, 18) (18, 18, 20, 20, 20) from the center back bind off sts,

and pick up and k9 towards the center of the left shoulder. Pm and join for working in the round [84 (84, 84, 84, 88) (88, 88, 92, 92, 92) sts].

Work in 1x1 ribbing for 4 inches (10 cm). Bind off loosely. Break the yarn, leaving a tail that is double the length of the neckband. Fold the bind off edge inwards and whip stitch the bind off edge to cast on edge.

FINISHING
Weave in any loose ends. Block your project using your preferred method.

WINTERBERRY SLIPOVER CABLE CHARTS

NOTE: Since Chart A is divided in half, this means you will need to read round/row 1 of Chart A (Right) before proceeding to round/row 1 of Chart A (Left).

Chart A (Left)

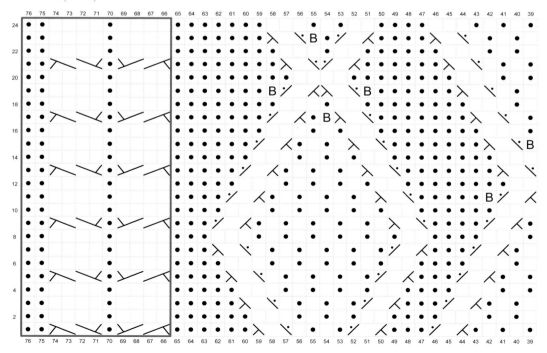

LEGEND

	☐	RS: K WS: P
	•	RS: P WS: K
	B	MB: (yo, k) 3 times into the next stitch. Turn work. Sl1wyif, p5. Turn work. Sl1wyib, k5. Turn work. (p2tog) 3 times. Turn work. Sl1wyib, k2tog, pass slipped st over the next st [1 st rem]
⟋	⟍	2/1 RPC: slip 1 st to cn and hold in back, k2, p1 from cn
⟍	⟍	2/1 LPC: slip 2 sts to cn and hold in front, p1, k2 from cn
⟍⟋	⟋⟍	2/2 RC: slip 2 sts to cn and hold in back, k2, k2 from cn
⟋⟍	⟋⟍	2/2 LC: slip 2 sts to cn and hold in front, k2, k2 from cn
	☐	Repeat section 0 (0, 1, 1, 2) (2, 2, 3, 3, 4) more times

Chart A (Right)

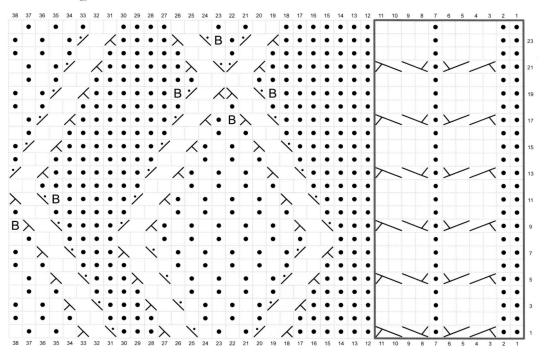

Ginger Zip

The Ginger Zip is a classic ribbed sweater with a literal twist. Casual yet sophisticated, this mockneck quarter zip features a relaxed silhouette and can be worn on its own or over layers on cooler days. The central cables draw your eyes up towards the neckline, which can be worn zipped or open with the collar down. Knit with a single strand of worsted weight wool for the ultimate stitch definition, this project is the perfect pattern to follow using your favorite workhorse yarn and will be a durable staple in your wardrobe for years to come.

Construction Notes

The sweater is worked from the bottom up in the round before separating for the front and back pieces. The front is further separated to create the zipper opening, with the collar stitches set aside for later. The shoulders are joined using a 3-needle bind off, and the collar is worked back and forth in rows. After binding off for the back collar, the fronts will be worked separately to create the zipper lining. Stitches are picked up for the armhole: German short rows are used to shape the sleeve cap, and the rest of the sleeve is worked in the round until the cuffs. Finally, the zipper is installed between the front collar and zipper lining pieces. **Note:** Due to the all-around ribbing, the sweater will appear smaller than expected before blocking.

SKILL LEVEL
Advanced

SIZING
XS (S, M, L, XL) (2XL, 3XL, 4XL, 5XL, 6XL)
40.75 (44.25, 47.5, 50.75, 57.5) (61.5, 64.75, 68.25, 71.5, 75)″ / 103.5 (112.5, 120.75, 129, 146) (156.25, 164.5, 173.25, 181.5, 190.5) cm, blocked

MATERIALS
Yarn
Worsted weight, Knit Picks Wool of the Andes Worsted in Mink Heather (100% Wool), 110 yds (101 m) per 50-g skein

Any worsted weight yarn can be used for this pattern as long as it matches gauge.

Yardage/Meterage
1105 (1190, 1390, 1420, 1505) (1590, 1695, 1800, 1910, 1990) yds / 1010 (1090, 1275, 1300, 1380) (1455, 1555, 1650, 1750, 1825) m of worsted weight yarn

Needles
For ribbing: US 6 (4 mm), 24- to 60-inch (60- to 150-cm) circular needles
For body and collar: US 8 (5 mm), 24- to 60-inch (60- to 150-cm) circular needles
For sleeves: US 8 (5 mm) double pointed needles

Notions
8″ (20-cm) closed bottom zipper
Cable needle
Scissors
Sewing needle and matching thread to sew the zipper
Stitch markers
Tapestry needle

GAUGE
25 sts x 32 rounds = 4 inches (10 cm) in 1x1 ribbing in the round using smaller needles (blocked)

19 sts x 26 rounds = 4 inches (10 cm) in 2x2 ribbing in the round using larger needles (blocked)

TECHNIQUES
3-Needle Bind Off (page 159)
German Short Rows (page 163)
Horizontal Invisible Seam (page 161)
Longtail Cast On (page 157)
Whip Stitch (page 162)
Zipper Installation (explained within the pattern)

ABBREVIATIONS

0 or -	no stitch / step does not apply to your size
1x1 ribbing	*k1, p1; repeat from * until end
BOR	beginning of round
cn	cable needle
DPN(s)	double pointed needle(s)
DS	double stitch
k	knit
k2tog	knit 2 sts together [1 st decreased]
MDS	make double stitch [see German short rows in Techniques (page 155)]
p	purl
patt	pattern
pm	place marker
rem	remain(ing)
RS	right side
sl1wyib	slip 1 st purlwise with yarn in back
sl1wyif	slip 1 st purlwise with yarn in front
sm	slip marker
ssk	slip 2 sts knitwise, one at a time; move both stitches back to the left needle; knit these 2 sts together through the back loops [1 st decreased]
st(s)	stitch(es)
stm	stitch marker
work(ing) even	continue working the pattern as established without any increases or decreases
WS	wrong side

Cable stitch abbreviations can be found in the Legend on page 31.

SCHEMATIC

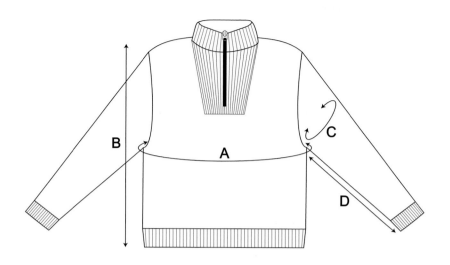

SIZING CHART

		XS	S	M	L	XL	2XL	3XL	4XL	5XL	6XL
A) Body circumference	in	40.75	44.25	47.5	50.75	57.5	61.5	64.75	68.25	71.5	75
	cm	103.5	112.5	120.75	129	146	156.25	164.5	173.25	181.5	190.5
B) Garment length	in	20.5	21	21.5	22	22.5	23	23.5	24	24.5	25
	cm	52	53.25	54.5	56	57.25	58.5	59.75	61	62.25	63.5
C) Sleeve circumference	in	15.25	15.25	16.75	16.75	20.25	20.25	23.5	23.5	23.5	25.25
	cm	38.5	38.5	42.5	42.5	51.5	51.5	60	60	60	64.25
D) Sleeve length	in	17	17	18	18.5	19	19.5	20	20.5	21	22
	cm	43.25	43.25	45.75	47	48.25	49.5	50.75	52	53.25	56

This sweater is designed with 9–13 inches (22.75–33 cm) of positive ease. Sample shown is knit in size XS.

GINGER ZIP PATTERN

BODY

Using US 6 (4 mm) needles, cast on 208 (224, 240, 256, 288) (312, 328, 344, 360, 376) sts using the longtail cast on method. Pm and join for working in the round.

Work in 1x1 ribbing for 2 inches (5 cm).

Switch to US 8 (5 mm) needles.

Set-up round 1: *P1, (k2, p2) 9 (10, 11, 12, 14) (14, 15, 16, 17, 18) times, work round 1 of Chart A (page 31), (p2, k2) 9 (10, 11, 12, 14) (14, 15, 16, 17, 18) times, p1; pm for side and repeat from * once more.

Set-up round 2: *P1, (k2, p2) 9 (10, 11, 12, 14) (14, 15, 16, 17, 18) times, work round 2 of Chart A, (p2, k2) 9 (10, 11, 12, 14) (14, 15, 16, 17, 18) times, p1; sm and repeat from * once more.

Continue working patt as established until the piece measures 13 inches (33 cm) from the cast on edge. Your last row should be an even numbered row.

Separate for Front/Back

Row 1 (RS): Remove BOR stm, bind off 4 (4, 4, 4, 6) (6, 6, 8, 8, 8) sts, work in patt until side stm. Remove stm and turn. Leave rem back sts on a holder or spare yarn to return to later [100 (108, 116, 124, 138) (150, 158, 164, 172, 180) sts rem].

TIP: Mark where you left off in the chart.

Row 2 (WS): Bind off 4 (4, 4, 4, 6) (6, 6, 8, 8, 8) sts, work in patt until end [96 (104, 112, 120, 132) (144, 152, 156, 164, 172) sts rem].
Row 3: K2, ssk, work in patt until last 4 sts, k2tog, k2 [94 (102, 110, 118, 130) (142, 150, 154, 162, 170) sts rem].
Row 4: Work in patt.
Repeat rows 3 and 4 a total of 3 (3, 3, 3, 5) (5, 5, 7, 7, 7) more times [88 (96, 104, 112, 120) (132, 140, 140, 148, 156) sts rem].

NOTE: There is an additional knit stitch intended for sleeve pickup.

Work even until the piece measures 14 (14.5, 15, 15.5, 16) (16.5, 17, 17.5, 18, 18.5) inches / 35.5 (36.75, 38, 39.25, 40.75) (42, 43.25, 44.5, 45.75, 47) cm from the cast on edge. Your last row should be a WS row.

Separate for Zipper Opening

Next row (RS): Work 27 (31, 35, 39, 43) (43, 47, 47, 51, 55) sts in patt, p1, pm, (k1, p1) 7 (7, 7, 7, 7) (10, 10, 10, 10, 10) times, k1, bind off 2 sts, (k1, p1) 7 (7, 7, 7, 7) (10, 10, 10, 10, 10) times, k1, pm, p1, work rem 27 (31, 35, 39, 43) (43, 47, 47, 51, 55) sts in patt. **Note:** The last bind off st counts as the first stitch of the ribbing. You should have 43 (47, 51, 55, 59) (65, 69, 69, 73, 77) sts on either side of the bind offs.

FRONT RIGHT

Leave front left sts on a holder or spare yarn to return to later.
Row 1 (WS): Work in patt until stm, sm, (p1, k1) 7 (7, 7, 7, 7) (10, 10, 10, 10, 10) times, p1.
Row 2 (RS): Sl1wyib, (p1, k1) until stm, sm, p1, k1, ssk, work in patt until end [42 (46, 50, 54, 58) (64, 68, 68, 72, 76) sts rem, 1 st decreased].
Row 3: Repeat row 1.
Row 4: Sl1wyib, (p1, k1) until stm, sm, work in patt until end.
Repeat the last 4 rows 3 (3, 7, 7, 7) (9, 9, 9, 9, 9) more times [39 (43, 43, 47, 51) (55, 59, 59, 63, 67) sts rem].

Work even until the piece measures 7.5 (8, 8.5, 9, 9.5) (10, 10.5, 11, 11.5, 12) inches / 19 (20.25, 21.5, 22.75, 24.25) (25.5, 26.75, 28, 29.25, 30.5) cm from the underarm bind off. Your last row should be a WS row. Break the yarn and move live sts to a holder or spare yarn to return to later, leaving the stm separating the collar from the shoulder.

FRONT LEFT

Rejoin the yarn to WS of work.

Row 1 (WS): Sl1wyif, (k1, p1) until stm, sm, work in patt until end.
Row 2 (RS): Work in patt until 4 sts before stm, k2tog, k1, p1, sm, (k1, p1) 7 (7, 7, 7, 7) (10, 10, 10, 10, 10) times, k1 [42 (46, 50, 54, 58) (64, 68, 68, 72, 76) sts rem, 1 st decreased].

Row 3: Repeat row 1.
Row 4: Work in patt until stm, sm, (k1, p1) 7 times, k1.
Repeat the last 4 rows 3 (3, 7, 7, 7) (9, 9, 9, 9, 9) more times [39 (43, 43, 47, 51) (55, 59, 59, 63, 67) sts rem].

Work even until the piece measures 7.5 (8, 8.5, 9, 9.5) (10, 10.5, 11, 11.5, 12) inches / 19 (20.25, 21.5, 22.75, 24.25) (25.5, 26.75, 28, 29.25, 30.5) cm from the underarm bind off. Your last row should be a WS row. Break the yarn and move live sts to a holder or spare yarn to return to later, leaving the stm separating the collar from the shoulder.

BACK

Rejoin the yarn to RS of work.

Row 1 (RS): Bind off 4 (4, 4, 4, 6) (6, 6, 8, 8, 8) sts, work in patt until end [100 (108, 116, 124, 138) (150, 158, 164, 172, 180) sts rem].
Row 2 (WS): Bind off 4 (4, 4, 4, 6) (6, 6, 8, 8, 8) sts, work in patt until end [96 (104, 112, 120, 132) (144, 152, 156, 164, 172) sts rem].
Row 3: K2, ssk, work in patt until last 4 sts, k2tog, k2 [94 (102, 110, 118, 130) (142, 150, 154, 162, 170) sts rem].
Row 4: Work in patt.
Repeat rows 3 and 4 a total of 3 (3, 3, 3, 5) (5, 5, 7, 7, 7) more times [88 (96, 104, 112, 120) (132, 140, 140, 148, 156) sts rem].

Work even until the piece measures 7.5 (8, 8.5, 9, 9.5) (10, 10.5, 11, 11.5, 12) inches / 19 (20.25, 21.5, 22.75, 24.25) (25.5, 26.75, 28, 29.25, 30.5) cm from the underarm bind off. Ensure the front and back pieces are the same length from the bottom of the ribbing.

COLLAR
Seaming Shoulders

Move live sts from the front pieces to a spare needle. Flip your work so the RSs are facing each other and position the pieces so the shoulder pieces are facing each other. Using the 3-needle bind off, bind off the shoulder sts until the stm and remove marker. Set aside the next 15 (15, 15, 15, 15) (21, 21, 21, 21, 21) collar sts on a holder or spare yarn to return to later. Continue binding off the 40 (40, 48, 48, 48) (64, 64, 64, 64, 64) sts from the back piece only. Set aside the other 15 (15, 15, 15, 15) (21, 21, 21, 21, 21) collar sts on a holder or spare yarn to return to later. Use the 3-needle bind off to bind off rem shoulder sts. Break the yarn and weave in any loose ends.

Begin with the right collar.

Row 1 (RS): Sl1wyib, (p1, k1) 7 (7, 7, 7, 7) (10, 10, 10, 10, 10) times, evenly pick up and k41 (41, 49, 49, 49) (65, 65, 65, 65, 65) sts across the back towards the other collar, (k1, p1) 7 (7, 7, 7, 7) (10, 10, 10, 10, 10) times, k1 [71 (71, 79, 79, 79) (107, 107, 107, 107, 107) sts]. **Note:** You will be picking up one additional st from the back relative to the bound off sts.
Row 2 (WS): Sl1wyif, (k1, p1) until end.
Row 3: Sl1wyib, (p1, k1) until end.

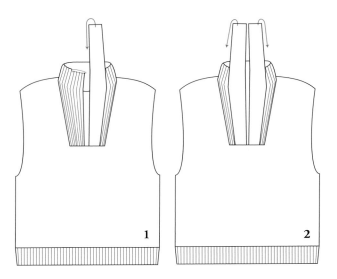

1   2

Work even until collar measures 5.5 inches (14 cm) from the back pick up edge. Your last row should be a WS row. The entire collar measured from the front split should be 11 inches (28 cm). Next, you will be binding off sts for the back of the collar and adding length to the front zipper lining pieces only. Once completed, the entire collar including the back neck will be folded along with the zipper lining.

Next row (RS): Sl1wyib, (p1, k1) 7 (7, 7, 7, 7) (10, 10, 10, 10, 10) times, bind off 41 (41, 49, 49, 49) (65, 65, 65, 65, 65) sts loosely, (k1, p1) 7 (7, 7, 7, 7) (10, 10, 10, 10, 10) times, k1. Turn. You will be working on the front left zipper lining first and setting aside the other side to return to later.

Front Left Zipper Lining
Row 1 (WS): Sl1wyif, (k1, p1) 7 (7, 7, 7, 7) (10, 10, 10, 10, 10) times.
Row 2 (RS): (K1, p1) 7 (7, 7, 7, 7) (10, 10, 10, 10, 10) times, k1.
Work even until zipper lining measures 5.5 inches (14 cm) from where you bound off for the back of the collar. Your last row should be a WS row. Bind off loosely. When folded, the bind off edge should meet the front zipper opening (image 1). Break the yarn, leaving a long 40-inch (101.5-cm) tail for seaming the lining to the collar, and then the bind off edge of the back collar to the pick up edge.

Front Right Zipper Lining
Rejoin the yarn to WS of work.

Row 1 (WS): (P1, k1) 7 (7, 7, 7, 7) (10, 10, 10, 10, 10) times, p1.
Row 2 (RS): Sl1wyib, (p1, k1) 7 (7, 7, 7, 7) (10, 10, 10, 10, 10) times.
Work even until zipper lining measures 5.25 inches (13.25 cm) from where you bound off for the back of the collar. Repeat row 1 one more time and bind off loosely (image 2). Break the yarn, leaving a 20-inch (50.75-cm) tail for seaming the lining to the collar.

SLEEVES (MAKE 2)

Using US 8 (5 mm) needles and beginning with the center of the underarm, pick up and k4 (4, 4, 4, 6) (6, 6, 8, 8, 8) from the bind off sts, pick up and k32 (32, 36, 36, 42) (42, 50, 48, 48, 52) towards the shoulder, pm, pick up and k32 (32, 36, 36, 42) (42, 50, 48, 48, 52) back down towards the underarm, and pick up and k4 (4, 4, 4, 6) (6, 6, 8, 8, 8) from the bind off sts. Pm and join for working in the round [72 (72, 80, 80, 96) (96, 112, 112, 112, 120) sts].

Short Row Shaping

Short row 1 (RS): P1, (k2, p2) until 1 st before stm, p1, sm, p1, (k2, p2) twice, turn.
Short row 2 (WS): MDS, work in patt until stm, sm, k1, (p2, k2) twice, turn.
Short row 3: MDS, work in patt until stm, sm, p1, (k2, p2) until 4 sts past DS (resolving existing DS), turn.
Short row 4: MDS, work in patt until stm, sm, k1, (p2, k2) until 4 sts past DS (resolving existing DS), turn.
Repeat the last 2 rows 5 (5, 7, 7, 7) (9, 9, 9, 9, 9) more times. In your final row, turn your work. MDS and work in patt until shoulder stm, remove marker and continue in patt until BOR stm, resolving DS along the way. You will be working in the round for the remainder of the sleeve.

Round 1: Work in patt until end, resolving the final DS as you come across it.
Round 2: P1, (k2, p2) until last st, p1.
Repeat the last round until the sleeve measures 6 (6, 6.5, 7, 7) (6.5, 6, 5.5, 5.5, 5) inches / 15.25 (15.25, 16.5, 17.75, 17.75) (16.5, 15.25, 14, 14, 12.75) cm from the underarm.

Decrease round: P1, k1, k2tog, work in patt until last 4 sts, ssk, k1, p1 [70 (70, 78, 78, 94) (94, 110, 110, 110, 118) sts rem, 2 sts decreased].

Switch to DPNs when necessary.

Repeat dec round every 6th (5th, 5th, 5th, 5th) (4th, 4th, 4th, 4th, 4th) round 3 more times, every 4th (4th, 4th, 4th, 4th) (4th, 3rd, 3rd, 3rd, 3rd) round 4 more times, every 0th (0th, 0th, 0th, 3rd) (3rd, 3rd, 3rd, 3rd, 3rd) round 4 more times, then every 0th (0th, 0th, 0th, 0th) (0th, 3rd, 3rd, 3rd, 3rd) round 8 more times [56 (56, 64, 64, 72) (72, 72, 72, 72, 80) sts rem].

Work even until the sleeve measures 15 (15, 16, 16.5, 17) (17.5, 18, 18.5, 19, 20) inches / 38 (38, 40.75, 42, 43.25) (44.5, 45.75, 47, 48.25, 50.75) cm from the underarm, or until it reaches the desired length.

To prepare for sewing, position the zipper so it is sandwiched between the two pieces of fabric. Use pins to secure it in place. Using your matching thread and beginning from the bottom, sew the zipper to the collar. Reinforce by sewing from the top down (image 3). Repeat on the other side.

Cuffs

Switch to US 6 (4 mm needles).

Decrease round: *K2, k2tog; repeat from * until end [42 (42, 48, 48, 54) (54, 54, 54, 54, 60) sts rem].

Work in 1x1 ribbing for 2 inches (5 cm). Bind off loosely in patt.

ZIPPER INSTALLATION

I recommend blocking your project prior to the zipper installation. Fold the collar inwards so the zipper lining sits behind the front collar band.

Right Zipper Lining Finishing

With your shorter yarn tail, whip stitch the bind off edge of the lining to the bottom of the front collar, and then up the side of the lining towards the bottom of the collar.

Left Zipper Lining Finishing

With your longer yarn tail, whip stitch the bind off edge of the lining to the bottom of the front collar, and then up the side of the lining towards the bottom of the collar.

Back Collar Finishing

Continuing with the tail from the left zipper lining, use the horizontal invisible seaming technique to seam the bind off edge of the collar to the pick up edge.

FINISHING

Weave in any loose ends.

GINGER ZIP CABLE CHART A

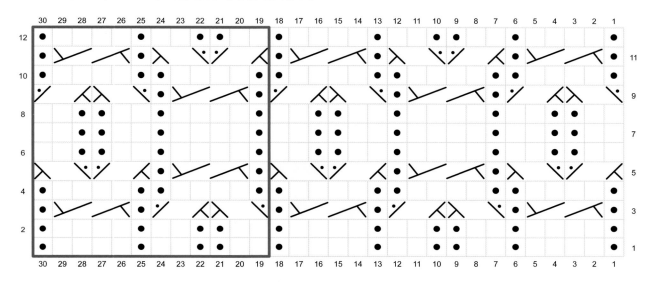

LEGEND

☐	RS: K WS: P
•	RS: P WS: K
⟋ ⟍	2/1 RPC: slip 1 st to cn and hold in back, k2, p1 from cn
⟍ ⟍	2/1 LPC: slip 2 sts to cn and hold in front, p1, k2 from cn
⟍⟋	2/2 RC: slip 2 sts to cn and hold in back, k2, k2 from cn
☐	Repeat section 0 (0, 0, 0, 0) (1, 1, 1, 1, 1) more times

Myrtle Tee

The Myrtle Tee is a modern reiteration of the classic collared shirt. With its meandering cables and oversized fit, this top is loosely inspired by the patterns found in vintage knitwear catalogues. Knit with wool and mohair yarns held together, the result is a fuzzy fabric that is both warm and breathable. The combination of yarns held at a looser gauge creates drape while the seams provide structure. The rib-knit collar, cuffs and hem add a professional touch to the garment. Whether worn with wide leg pants for a day at the office or styled under a corduroy blazer for a more formal occasion, the possibilities for dressing up or down are endless.

Construction Notes

The tee is worked flat from the bottom up in rectangular panels. The front piece separates at the center, with the left and right sides worked separately to create the front opening. The back piece is nearly identical but is worked without the collar shaping. Once both panels are complete, the sides and shoulders are seamed. Stitches are picked up along the V-neck opening and a folded hem is created on each side for a clean edge. Once the edge is complete, stitches are picked up around the neck opening and worked back and forth for the collar. Finally, stitches are picked up in the round for the sleeves.

SKILL LEVEL
Intermediate

SIZING
XS (S, M, L, XL) (2XL, 3XL, 4XL, 5XL, 6XL)
38.5 (42.5, 46.5, 50.5, 54.5) (58.5, 62.5, 66.5, 70.5, 74.5)" / 97.75 (108, 118, 128.25, 138.5) (148.5, 158.75, 169, 179, 189.25) cm, blocked

MATERIALS
Yarn
DK weight, DROPS Lima in Ice Blue (65% Wool, 35% Alpaca), 109 yds (100 m) per 50-g skein
held with
Lace weight, DROPS Kid-Silk in 7 (75% Mohair, 25% Silk), 230 yds (210 m) per 25-g skein

Any DK and lace weight yarn held together can be used for this pattern as long as it matches gauge. If using a single strand of yarn, any worsted weight yarn can be used as long as it matches gauge.

Yardage/Meterage
765 (805, 875, 1040, 1145) (1255, 1310, 1375, 1435, 1475) yds / 700 (735, 800, 950, 1050) (1150, 1200, 1260, 1315, 1350) m of DK weight yarn *held with*
765 (805, 875, 1040, 1145) (1255, 1310, 1375, 1435, 1475) yds / 700 (735, 800, 950, 1050) (1150, 1200, 1260, 1315, 1350) m of lace weight yarn

Needles
For ribbing: US 8 (5 mm), 24- to 60-inch (60- to 150-cm) circular needles
For body: US 9 (5.5 mm), 24- to 60-inch (60- to 150-cm) circular needles
For collar: US 6 (4 mm), 16- to 24-inch (40- to 60-cm) circular needles

Notions
Cable needle
Scissors
Stitch markers
Tapestry needle

GAUGE
22 sts x 21 rows = 4 inches (10 cm) in Chart A worked flat using largest needles (blocked)

23 sts x 21 rows = 4 inches (10 cm) in Chart B worked flat using largest needles (blocked)

TECHNIQUES
Horizontal Invisible Seam (page 161)
Longtail Cast On (page 157)
Whip Stitch (page 162)

ABBREVIATIONS

0 or -	no stitch / step does not apply to your size
1x1 ribbing	*k1, p1; repeat from * repeat until end
cn	cable needle
inc	increase
k	knit
k2tog	knit 2 sts together [1 st decreased]
m1pl	make 1 left leaning purl increase: Use the left needle to pick up the strand between the last worked st and the next unworked st from front to back; purl this st through the back loop [1 st increased]
m1pr	make 1 right leaning purl increase: Use the left needle to pick up the strand between the last worked st and the next unworked st from back to front; purl this st through the front loop [1 st increased]
p	purl
p2tog	purl 2 sts together [1 st decreased]
patt	pattern
pm	place marker
rem	remain(ing)
RS	right side
sl1wyib	slip 1 st purlwise with yarn in back
sl1wyif	slip 1 st purlwise with yarn in front
sm	slip marker
ssk	slip 2 sts knitwise, one at a time; move both stitches back to the left needle; knit these 2 sts together through the back loops [1 st decreased]
ssp	slip 2 sts knitwise, one at a time; move both stitches back to the left needle; purl these 2 sts together through the back loops [1 st decreased]
st(s)	stitch(es)
stm	stitch marker
work(ing) even	continue working the pattern as established without any increases or decreases
WS	wrong side

Cable stitch abbreviations can be found in the Legends on pages 40–44.

SCHEMATIC

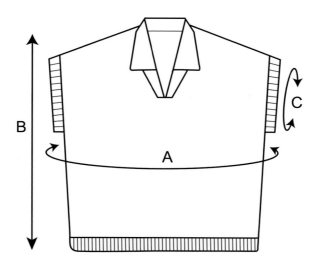

SIZING CHART

		XS	S	M	L	XL	2XL	3XL	4XL	5XL	6XL
A) Body circumference	in	38.5	42.5	46.5	50.5	54.5	58.5	62.5	66.5	70.5	74.5
	cm	97.75	108	118	128.25	138.5	148.5	158.75	169	179	189.25
B) Garment length	in	21	21	21.5	21.5	22	22	23	23	23.5	23.5
	cm	53.25	53.25	54.5	54.5	56	56	58.5	58.5	59.75	59.75
C) Sleeve circumference	in	15	16	17.25	18.5	20	20.75	21.75	22.5	23.5	24.25
	cm	38	40.75	43.75	47	50.75	52.75	55.25	57.25	59.75	61.5

This tee is designed with 8.5–10.5 inches (21.5–26.75 cm) of positive ease. Sample shown is knit in size XS.

MYRTLE TEE PATTERN

FRONT

Using US 8 (5 mm) needles, cast on 94 (98, 102, 118, 126) (146, 150, 154, 174, 178) sts using the longtail cast on method.

Work in 1x1 ribbing for 1.5 inches (3.75 cm), ending on a WS row.

Switch to US 9 (5.5 mm) needles.

Set-up row 1 (RS): P5 (7, 9, 3, 7) (3, 5, 7, 3, 5), pm, work row 1 of Chart A (page 40) 0 (0, 0, 1, 1) (2, 2, 2, 3, 3) times, work row 1 of Chart B (page 41), work row 1 of Chart C (page 42), work row 1 of Chart D (page 43), work row 1 of Chart E (page 44) 0 (0, 0, 1, 1) (2, 2, 2, 3, 3) times, pm, p5 (7, 9, 3, 7) (3, 5, 7, 3, 5).
Set-up row 2 (WS): K5 (7, 9, 3, 7) (3, 5, 7, 3, 5), sm, work row 2 of Chart E 0 (0, 0, 1, 1) (2, 2, 2, 3, 3) times, work row 2 of Chart D, work row 2 of Chart C, work row 2 of Chart B, work row 2 of Chart A 0 (0, 0, 1, 1) (2, 2, 2, 3, 3) times, sm, k5 (7, 9, 3, 7) (3, 5, 7, 3, 5).

Continue working patt as established until the piece measures 3 inches (7.5 cm) from the cast on edge. Your last row should be a WS row.

Next row (RS, inc): P1, m1pr, p until stm, sm, work next row of all charts as established, sm, p until last st, m1pl, p1 [96 (100, 104, 120, 128) (148, 152, 156, 176, 180) sts].

Repeat inc row every 6th (6th, 4th, 4th, 4th) (4th, 4th, 4th, 4th, 4th) row a total of 2 (4, 6, 6, 6) (4, 6, 8, 6, 8) more times [100 (108, 116, 132, 140) (156, 164, 172, 188, 196) sts].

Continue working the pattern and charts as established until the piece measures 13.5 (13.5, 14, 14, 14.5) (14.5, 15, 15, 16, 17) inches / 34.25 (34.25, 35.5, 35.5, 36.75) (36.75, 38, 38, 40.75, 43.25) cm from the cast on edge. Your last row should be a WS row.

Separate for Collar

Next row (RS): Work 47 (51, 55, 63, 67) (75, 79, 83, 91, 95) sts in patt, bind off 6 sts, work rem 47 (51, 55, 63, 67) (75, 79, 83, 91, 95) sts in patt. Leave front left sts on a holder or spare yarn to return to later.

TIP: Mark where you left off in the chart.

FRONT RIGHT

Beginning with a WS row, work even until the piece measures 17 (17, 17.5, 17.5, 18) (18, 18.5, 18.5, 19.5, 20.5) inches / 43.25 (43.25, 44.5, 44.5, 45.75) (45.75, 47, 47, 49.5, 52) cm from the cast on edge. Your last row should be a WS row.

Row 1 (RS): Bind off 5 (5, 5, 5, 6) (6, 6, 7, 7, 7) sts, work in patt until end [42 (46, 50, 58, 61) (69, 73, 76, 84, 88) sts rem].
Row 2 (WS): Work in patt.
Row 3: K1, ssk, work in patt until end [41 (45, 49, 57, 60) (68, 72, 75, 83, 87) sts rem].
Row 4: Repeat row 2.
Repeat the last 2 rows a total of 10 more times [31 (35, 39, 47, 50) (58, 62, 65, 73, 77) sts rem].

Work even until the piece measures 21 (21, 21.5, 21.5, 22) (22, 23, 23, 23.5, 23.5) inches / 53.25 (53.25, 54.5, 54.5, 56) (56, 58.5, 58.5, 59.75, 59.75) cm from the cast on edge. Your last row should be a WS row.

Next row (RS): K1, p2tog, work in patt until end [30 (34, 38, 46, 49) (57, 61, 64, 72, 76) sts rem].
Next row (WS): Bind off 10 (12, 13, 16, 17) (19, 21, 22, 24, 26) sts, work in patt until end [20 (22, 25, 30, 32) (38, 40, 42, 48, 50) sts rem].
Next row: Work in patt.
Next row: Bind off 10 (12, 13, 16, 17) (19, 21, 22, 24, 26) sts, work in patt until end [10 (10, 12, 14, 15) (19, 19, 20, 24, 24) sts rem].
Next row: Work in patt.
Next row: Bind off rem 10 (10, 12, 14, 15) (19, 19, 20, 24, 24) sts.

Break the yarn, leaving a tail that is double the length of the shoulder for seaming.

FRONT LEFT

Rejoin the yarn to WS of work and work even until the piece measures 17 (17, 17.5, 17.5, 18) (18, 18.5, 18.5, 19.5, 20.5) inches / 43.25 (43.25, 44.5, 44.5, 45.75) (45.75, 47, 47, 49.5, 52) cm from the cast on edge. Your last row should be a RS row.

Row 1 (WS): Bind off 5 (5, 5, 5, 6) (6, 6, 7, 7, 7) sts, work in patt until end [42 (46, 50, 58, 61) (69, 73, 76, 84, 88) sts rem].
Row 2 (RS): Work in patt until last 3 sts, k2tog, k1 [41 (45, 49, 57, 60) (68, 72, 75, 83, 87) sts rem].
Row 3: Work in patt.
Row 4: Repeat row 2 [40 (44, 48, 56, 59) (67, 71, 74, 82, 86) sts rem].
Repeat the last 2 rows a total of 9 more times [31 (35, 39, 47, 50) (58, 62, 65, 73, 77) sts rem].

Work one more WS row in patt.

Work even until the piece measures 21 (21, 21.5, 21.5, 22) (22, 23, 23, 23.5, 23.5) inches / 53.25 (53.25, 54.5, 54.5, 56) (56, 58.5, 58.5, 59.75, 59.75) cm from the cast on edge. Your last row should be a WS row.

Next row (RS): Work in patt until last 3 sts, ssp, k1 [30 (34, 38, 46, 49) (57, 61, 64, 72, 76) sts rem].
Next row (WS): Work in patt.
Next row: Bind off 10 (12, 13, 16, 17) (19, 21, 22, 24, 26) sts, work in patt until end [20 (22, 25, 30, 32) (38, 40, 42, 48, 50) sts rem].
Next row: Work in patt.
Next row: Bind off 10 (12, 13, 16, 17) (19, 21, 22, 24, 26) sts, work in patt until end [10 (10, 12, 14, 15) (19, 19, 20, 24, 24) sts rem].
Next row: Bind off rem 10 (10, 12, 14, 15) (19, 19, 20, 24, 24) sts.

Break the yarn, leaving a tail that is double the length of the shoulder for seaming.

BACK

Using US 8 (5 mm) needles, cast on 94 (98, 102, 118, 126) (146, 150, 154, 174, 178) sts using the longtail cast on method.

Work in 1x1 ribbing for 1.5 inches (3.75 cm), ending on a WS row.

Switch to US 9 (5.5 mm) needles.

Set-up row 1 (RS): P5 (7, 9, 3, 7) (3, 5, 7, 3, 5), pm, work row 1 of Chart A 0 (0, 0, 1, 1) (2, 2, 2, 3, 3) times, work row 1 of Chart B, work row 1 of Chart C, work row 1 of Chart D, work row 1 of Chart E 0 (0, 0, 1, 1) (2, 2, 2, 3, 3) times, pm, p5 (7, 9, 3, 7) (3, 5, 7, 3, 5).

Set-up row 2 (WS): K5 (7, 9, 3, 7) (3, 5, 7, 3, 5), sm, work row 2 of Chart E 0 (0, 0, 1, 1) (2, 2, 2, 3, 3) times, work row 2 of Chart D, work row 2 of Chart C, work row 2 of Chart B, work row 2 of Chart A 0 (0, 0, 1, 1) (2, 2, 2, 3, 3) times, sm, k5 (7, 9, 3, 7) (3, 5, 7, 3, 5).

Continue working patt as established until the piece measures 3 inches (7.5 cm) from the cast on edge. Your last row should be a WS row.

Next row (RS, inc): P1, m1pr, p until stm, sm, work next row of all charts as established, sm, p until last st, m1pl, p1 [96 (100, 104, 120, 128) (148, 152, 156, 176, 180) sts].

Repeat inc row every 6th (6th, 4th, 4th, 4th) (4th, 4th, 4th, 4th, 4th) a total of 2 (4, 6, 6, 6) (4, 6, 8, 6, 8) more times [100 (108, 116, 132, 140) (156, 164, 172, 188, 196) sts].

Work even until the piece measures 21 (21, 21.5, 21.5, 22) (22, 23, 23, 23.5, 23.5) inches / 53.25 (53.25, 54.5, 54.5, 56) (56, 58.5, 58.5, 59.75, 59.75) cm from the cast on edge. Your last row should be a WS row.

Next 4 rows: Bind off 10 (12, 13, 16, 17) (19, 21, 22, 24, 26) sts, work in patt until end [60 (60, 64, 68, 72) (80, 80, 84, 92, 92) sts rem].
Next 2 rows: Bind off 10 (10, 12, 14, 15) (19, 19, 20, 24, 24) sts, work in patt until end [40 (40, 40, 40, 42) (42, 42, 44, 44, 44) sts rem].

Bind off rem 40 (40, 40, 40, 42) (42, 42, 44, 44, 44) sts.

V-NECK EDGING
With the WS of the front and back pieces facing each other, use a tapestry needle and the horizontal invisible seaming technique to seam the shoulders.

Switch to US 6 (4 mm) needles for the V-neck ribbing.

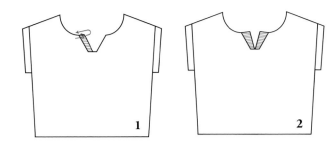

Right side
With the RS facing you and beginning with the bottom of the V-neck, evenly pick up and k16 (16, 16, 16, 16) (18, 18, 18, 18, 18) up towards the collar bind off. Turn.

Next row (WS): *K1, p1; repeat from * until end. Repeat the last row until the ribbing measures 1.75 inches (4.5 cm) from the pick up edge. Your last row should be a RS row.

Bind off, leaving a tail that is double the length of the V-neck edge. Fold the ribbing inwards and whip stitch the bind off edge to the pick up edge (image 1). Use the remainder of the tail to seam the edge of the ribbing to half of the bind off edge at the bottom of the V-neck.

Left Side
With the RS facing you and beginning with the collar bind off edge, evenly pick up and k16 (16, 16, 16, 16) (18, 18, 18, 18, 18) down towards the V-neck bind off. Turn.

Next row (WS): *K1, p1; repeat from * until end. Repeat the last row until the ribbing measures 1.75 inches (4.5 cm) from the pick up edge. Your last row should be a WS row.

Bind off, leaving a tail that is double the length of the V-neck edge. Fold the ribbing inwards and whip stitch the bind off edge to the pick up edge (image 2). Use the remainder of the tail to seam the edge of the ribbing to the other half of the bind off edge at the bottom of the V-neck.

COLLAR

Using US 6 (4 mm) needles and beginning with the front right collar edge, pick up and k5 from the top edge of the right V-neck ribbing, pick up and k5 (5, 5, 5, 6) (6, 6, 7, 7, 7) from the front right bind off sts, evenly pick up and k28 (28, 29, 29, 30) (30, 31, 31, 32, 33) towards the right shoulder, pick up and k40 (40, 40, 40, 42) (42, 42, 44, 44, 44) from the back bind off sts, evenly pick up and k28 (28, 29, 29, 30) (30, 31, 31, 32, 33) towards the front, pick up and k5 (5, 5, 5, 6) (6, 6, 7, 7, 7) from the front left bind off sts, and pick up and k5 from the top edge of the left V-neck ribbing. Turn [116 (116, 118, 118, 124) (124, 126, 130, 132, 134) sts].

Next row (WS): Sl1wyib, p1, (k1, p1) until end. Repeat the last row until collar measures 4 inches (10 cm) from the pick up edge (image 3). Bind off in patt.

SLEEVE RIBBING (MAKE 2)

Using a tapestry needle and the vertical invisible seaming technique, seam the sides from the cast on ribbing up towards the shoulder, leaving an arm opening 7.5 (8, 8.5, 9, 9.5) (10, 10.5, 11, 11.5, 12) inches / 19 (20.25, 21.5, 22.75, 24.25) (25.5, 26.75, 28, 29.25, 30.5) cm long under the shoulder seam.

Using US 6 (4 mm) needles and beginning at the center of the underarm, evenly pick up and k36 (38, 41, 44, 47) (49, 51, 53, 55, 57) towards the shoulder, then evenly pick up and k36 (38, 41, 44, 47) (49, 51, 53, 55, 57) back towards the under-arm. Pm and join for working in the round [72 (76, 82, 88, 94) (98, 102, 106, 110, 114) sts].

Work in 1x1 ribbing for 1.75 inches (4.5 cm).

Bind off loosely, leaving a tail that is double the circumference of the sleeve opening. Fold the sleeve ribbing inwards and whip stitch the bind off edge to the pick up edge.

FINISHING

Weave in any loose ends. Block your project using your preferred method.

MYRTLE TEE CABLE CHARTS AND LEGENDS

Chart A

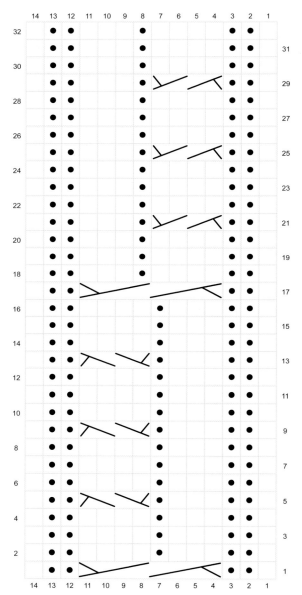

Legend A

☐	RS: K WS: P
•	RS: P WS: K
	2/2 RC: slip 2 sts to cn and hold in back, k2, k2 from cn
	2/2 LC: slip 2 sts to cn and hold in front, k2, k2 from cn
	4/4 RC: slip 4 sts to cn and hold in back, k4, k4 from cn
	4/4 LC: slip 4 sts to cn and hold in front, k4, k4 from cn

Chart B

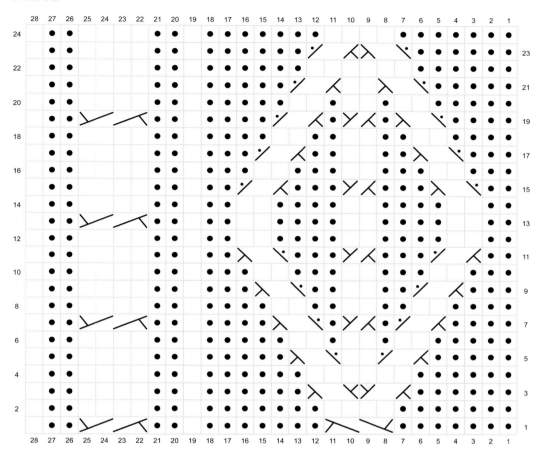

Legend B

(blank)	RS: K / WS: P
•	RS: P / WS: K
Y↗	1/1 RC: slip 1 st to cn and hold in back, k1, k1 from cn
·↗	2/1 RPC: slip 1 st to cn and hold in back, k2, p1 from cn
↘ ·	2/1 LPC: slip 2 sts to cn and hold in front, p1, k2 from cn
Y↗	2/1 RC: slip 1 st to cn and hold in back, k2, k1 from cn
↘ ↗	2/1 LC: slip 2 sts to cn and hold in front, k1, k2 from cn
↙↗	2/2 RC: slip 2 sts to cn and hold in back, k2, k2 from cn
↘↙	2/2 LC: slip 2 sts to cn and hold in front, k2, k2 from cn

Chart C

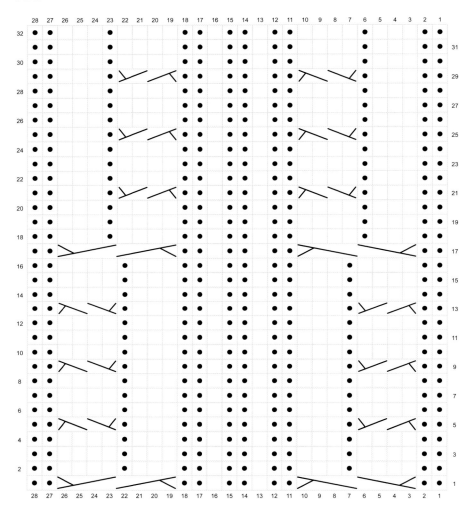

Legend C

	RS: K WS: P
•	RS: P WS: K
2/2 RC	2/2 RC: slip 2 sts to cn and hold in back, k2, k2 from cn
2/2 LC	2/2 LC: slip 2 sts to cn and hold in front, k2, k2 from cn

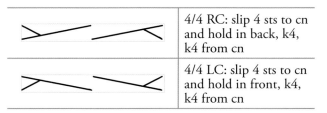

	4/4 RC: slip 4 sts to cn and hold in back, k4, k4 from cn
	4/4 LC: slip 4 sts to cn and hold in front, k4, k4 from cn

Chart D

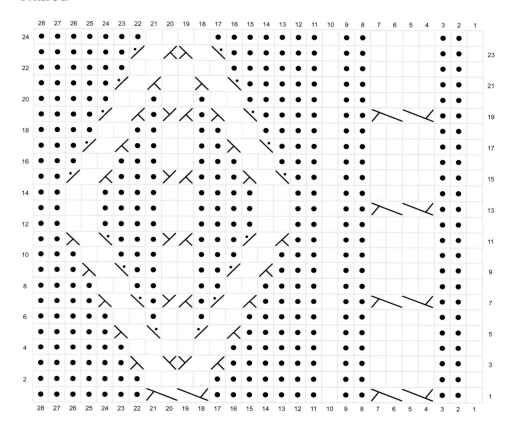

Legend D

(blank)	RS: K WS: P	⅄ ⤡	2/1 LPC: slip 2 sts to cn and hold in front, p1, k2 from cn
•	RS: P WS: K	⅄ ⋏	2/1 RC: slip 1 st to cn and hold in back, k2, k1 from cn
⅄⋏	1/1 RC: slip 1 st to cn and hold in back, k1, k1 from cn	⅄ ⋏	2/1 LC: slip 2 sts to cn and hold in front, k1, k2 from cn
⤢ ⋏	2/1 RPC: slip 1 st to cn and hold in back, k2, p1 from cn	⟋⟍	2/2 LC: slip 2 sts to cn and hold in front, k2, k2 from cn

Chart E

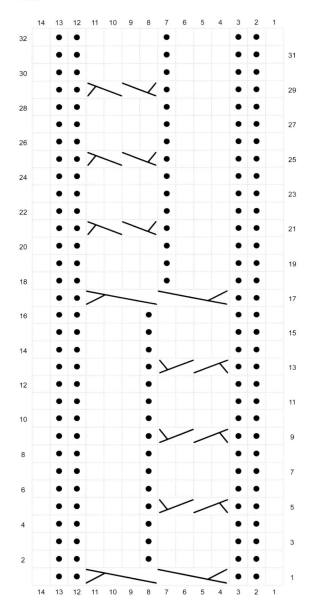

Legend E

☐	RS: K WS: P
●	RS: P WS: K
╲╱	2/2 RC: slip 2 sts to cn and hold in back, k2, k2 from cn
╲╱	2/2 LC: slip 2 sts to cn and hold in front, k2, k2 from cn
╲╱	4/4 RC: slip 4 sts to cn and hold in back, k4, k4 from cn
╲╱	4/4 LC: slip 4 sts to cn and hold in front, k4, k4 from cn

Juniper Vest

Sweater vests are a fall essential, and the Juniper Vest is no exception. Designed as a layer-ready garment, the result is an oversized V-neck cabled vest with just the right amount of room and drape. Bobbles, twists and diamond cables provide endless texture from top to bottom. The vest can be slipped comfortably over a dress shirt for a casual-chic pairing. Leave the collar unbuttoned and peeking out of the V-neck for the perfect mix of sophistication and streetstyle. The split hem allows for easier movement and versatility in styling the bottom half of your outfit. Complete the ensemble with a simple pair of leggings and sneakers or elevate the look with faux leather pants and stilettos. The relaxed and slouchy fit means you can be creative in mixing and matching pieces, creating countless outfits to wear all year long.

Construction Notes

The vest begins with a split hem that is knit separately, after which the pieces are joined and the cable patterns are worked in the round until the armhole openings. The front and back pieces are knit flat separately, and the shoulders are joined using a 3-needle bind off. Stitches are picked up for the neckline, and mitred decreases are worked to shape the V-neck. Finally, stitches are picked up and worked for the armhole edges.

SKILL LEVEL
Intermediate

SIZING
XS (S, M, L, XL) (2XL, 3XL, 4XL, 5XL, 6XL)
36.5 (40.5, 44.5, 48.5, 52.5) (56.5, 60.5, 64.5, 68.5, 72.5)" / 92.75 (102.75, 113, 123.25, 133.25) (143.5, 153.75, 163.75, 174, 184.25) cm, blocked

MATERIALS
Yarn
Worsted weight, Knitting for Olive Heavy Merino in Mushroom Rose (100% Merino Wool), 137 yds (125 m) per 50-g skein

Any worsted weight yarn can be used for this pattern as long as it matches gauge.

Yardage/Meterage
710 (860, 875, 915, 955) (1010, 1065, 1130, 1185, 1310) yds / 650 (785, 800, 835, 875) (925, 975, 1035, 1085, 1200) m of worsted weight yarn

Needles
For ribbing: US 6 (4 mm), 24- to 60-inch (60- to 150-cm) circular needles
For body: US 8 (5 mm), 24- to 60-inch (60- to 150-cm) circular needles

Notions
Cable needle
Scissors
Stitch markers
Tapestry needle

GAUGE
20 sts x 25 rounds = 4 inches (10 cm) in moss stitch in the round using larger needles (blocked)

TECHNIQUES
3-Needle Bind Off (page 159)
Longtail Cast On (page 157)

ABBREVIATIONS

0 or -	no stitch / step does not apply to your size
1x1 ribbing	*k1, p1; repeat from * repeat until end
BOR	beginning of round
CDD	centered double decrease: slip 2 sts together knitwise; knit 1 st; using the tip of your left needle, pick up the 2 sts you slipped and pass them over the knitted st and off of the needle [2 sts decreased]
cn	cable needle
k	knit
k1tbl	knit through the back loop
k2tog	knit two stitches together [1 st decreased]
p	purl
p2tog	purl 2 sts together [1 st decreased]
patt	pattern
pm	place marker
rem	remain(ing)
RS	right side
sl1wyib	slip 1 st purlwise with yarn in back
sl1wyif	slip 1 st purlwise with yarn in front
st(s)	stitch(es)
stm	stitch marker
work(ing) even	continue working the pattern as established without any increases or decreases
WS	wrong side
yo	yarnover

Cable stitch abbreviations can be found in the Legends on pages 52–53.

SCHEMATIC

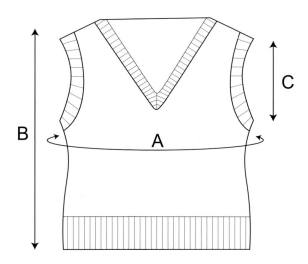

SIZING CHART

		XS	S	M	L	XL	2XL	3XL	4XL	5XL	6XL
A) Body circumference	in	36.5	40.5	44.5	48.5	52.5	56.5	60.5	64.5	68.5	72.5
	cm	92.75	102.75	113	123.25	133.25	143.5	153.75	163.75	174	184.25
B) Garment length	in	20.75	21.25	21.75	22.25	22.75	23.25	23.75	24.25	24.75	25.25
	cm	52.75	54	55.25	56.5	57.75	59	60.25	61.5	62.75	64.25
C) Armhole depth	in	8.75	9.25	9.75	10.25	10.75	11.25	11.75	12.25	12.75	13.25
	cm	22.25	23.5	24.75	26	27.25	28.5	29.75	31	32.5	33.75

This vest is designed with 6.5–8.5 inches (16.5–21.5 cm) of positive ease. Sample shown is knit in size XS.

JUNIPER VEST PATTERN

BACK RIBBING

Using US 6 (4 mm) needles, cast on 108 (118, 126, 134, 142) (150, 158, 166, 176, 184) sts using the longtail cast on method.

Row 1: Sl1wyib, (p1, k1) until last st, p1. Repeat the last row until ribbing measures 3 inches (7.5 cm) from the cast on edge, ending on a WS row. Break the yarn and set aside on a holder or spare yarn to return to later.

FRONT RIBBING

Using US 6 (4 mm) needles, cast on 108 (118, 126, 134, 142) (150, 158, 166, 176, 184) sts using the longtail cast on method.

Row 1: Sl1wyib, (p1, k1) until last st, p1. Repeat the last row until ribbing measures 3 inches (7.5 cm) from the cast on edge, ending on a WS row.

Repeat row 1 once more.

After that row is complete, pm for side, and continue working (k1, p1) across the back ribbing you had previously set aside. Pm and join for working in the round [216 (236, 252, 268, 284) (300, 316, 332, 352, 368) sts].

Switch to US 8 (5 mm) needles.

Round 1: *P6 (6, 10, 14, 14) (18, 18, 22, 22, 26), work round 1 of Chart A (page 52), work round 1 of Chart B (page 53), work round 1 of Chart A, p6 (6, 10, 14, 14) (18, 18, 22, 22, 26); repeat from * once more.
Round 2: *P6 (6, 10, 14, 14) (18, 18, 22, 22, 26), work round 2 of Chart A, work round 2 of Chart B, work round 2 of Chart A, p6 (6, 10, 14, 14) (18, 18, 22, 22, 26); repeat from * once more.

Continue working in patt as established until the piece measures 11 inches (28 cm) from the cast on edge. Your last row should be an even numbered row.

Separate for Front/Back

Row 1 (RS): Remove BOR stm, bind off 3 (3, 3, 4, 4) (4, 5, 5, 5, 6) sts, work in patt until side stm. Remove side marker and turn. Leave rem back sts on a holder or spare yarn to return to later [105 (115, 123, 130, 138) (146, 153, 161, 171, 178) sts rem].

TIP: Mark where you left off in the charts.

Row 2 (WS): Bind off 3 (3, 3, 4, 4) (4, 5, 5, 5, 6) sts, work in patt until end [102 (112, 120, 126, 134) (142, 148, 156, 166, 172) sts rem].
Row 3: Bind off 1 st, work in patt until end [101 (111, 119, 125, 133) (141, 147, 155, 165, 171) sts rem].
Row 4: Bind off 1 st, work in patt until end [100 (110, 118, 124, 132) (140, 146, 154, 164, 170) sts rem].
Repeat the last 2 rows a total of 1 (1, 2, 3, 3) (4, 4, 5, 5, 6) more time(s) [98 (108, 114, 118, 126) (132, 138, 144, 154, 158) sts rem].

FRONT LEFT

Row 1 (RS): Work in patt for 49 (54, 57, 59, 63) (66, 69, 72, 77, 79) sts, turn. Leave front right sts on a holder or spare yarn to return to later.

TIP: Mark where you left off in the charts.

Row 2 (WS): Bind off 1 st, work in patt until end.
Row 3: Work in patt.
Repeat the last 2 rows a total of 23 (26, 26, 26, 27) (27, 27, 28, 29, 29) more times [25 (27, 30, 32, 35) (38, 41, 43, 47, 49) sts rem].

NOTE: If you reach a point where there are not enough sts to complete a cable pattern because part of it has been bound off, k the remaining sts instead.

FRONT RIGHT

Rejoin the yarn to RS of work.

Row 1 (RS): Bind off 1 st, work in patt until end.
Row 2 (WS): Work in patt.
Repeat the last 2 rows a total of 23 (26, 26, 26, 27) (27, 27, 28, 29, 29) more times [25 (27, 30, 32, 35) (38, 41, 43, 47, 49) sts rem].

Work even until the front right measures 20.75 (21.25, 21.75, 22.25, 22.75) (23.25, 23.75, 24.25, 24.75, 25.25) inches / 52.75 (54, 55.25, 56.5, 57.75) (59, 60.25, 61.5, 62.75, 64.25) cm from the cast on edge. Your last row should be a WS row and match where you left off in the front left piece. Break the yarn and move live sts to a holder or spare yarn to return to later.

BACK

Rejoin the yarn to RS of work.

Row 1 (RS): Bind off 3 (3, 3, 4, 4) (4, 5, 5, 5, 6) sts, work in patt until end [105 (115, 123, 130, 138) (146, 153, 161, 171, 178) sts rem].
Row 2 (WS): Bind off 3 (3, 3, 4, 4) (4, 5, 5, 5, 6) sts, work in patt until end [102 (112, 120, 126, 134) (142, 148, 156, 166, 172) sts rem].
Row 3: Bind off 1 st, work in patt until end [101 (111, 119, 125, 133) (141, 147, 155, 165, 171) sts rem].
Row 4: Bind off 1 st, work in patt until end [100 (110, 118, 124, 132) (140, 146, 154, 164, 170) sts rem].
Repeat the last 2 rows a total of 1 (1, 2, 3, 3) (4, 4, 5, 5, 6) more time(s) [98 (108, 114, 118, 126) (132, 138, 144, 154, 158) sts rem].

Work even until the piece measures 20.75 (21.25, 21.75, 22.25, 22.75) (23.25, 23.75, 24.25, 24.75, 25.25) inches / 52.75 (54, 55.25, 56.5, 57.75) (59, 60.25, 61.5, 62.75, 64.25) cm from the cast on edge. Your last row should be a WS row and match where you left off in the front pieces.

Work even until the front left measures 20.75 (21.25, 21.75, 22.25, 22.75) (23.25, 23.75, 24.25, 24.75, 25.25) inches / 52.75 (54, 55.25, 56.5, 57.75) (59, 60.25, 61.5, 62.75, 64.25) cm from the cast on edge. Your last row should be a WS row. Break the yarn and move live sts to a holder or spare yarn to return to later.

Flip your work so the RSs are facing each other and place your front left and right live sts on another US 8 (5 mm) needle.

Using the 3-needle bind off method, bind off 25 (27, 30, 32, 35) (38, 41, 43, 47, 49) sts from the front right sts. Bind off the 48 (54, 54, 54, 56) (56, 56, 58, 60, 60) back neck edge sts, and 3-needle bind off 25 (27, 30, 32, 35) (38, 41, 43, 47, 49) sts from the front left sts.

NECKBAND
Flip work so the RSs are facing out. Using US 6 (4 mm) needles and beginning with the left shoulder, evenly pick up and k52 (58, 58, 58, 60) (60, 60, 62, 64, 64) towards the center front, pick up and k1 and place a removable stm in this st, evenly pick up and k52 (58, 58, 58, 60) (60, 60, 62, 64, 64) towards the right shoulder, and pick up and k49 (55, 55, 55, 57) (57, 57, 59, 61, 61) back sts [154 (172, 172, 172, 178) (178, 178, 184, 190, 190) sts].

Round 1: Work in 1x1 ribbing until 1 st before center stm, CDD, continue in 1x1 ribbing until end of round.
Repeat round 1 until ribbing measures 1 inch (2.5 cm) from the pick up edge. Bind off in patt and remove markers.

ARMHOLE EDGE (MAKE 2)
Using US 6 (4 mm) needles and beginning with the center of the underarm, pick up and k3 (3, 3, 4, 4) (4, 5, 5, 5, 6) from the bind off sts, evenly pick up and k49 (53, 57, 61, 65) (69, 73, 77, 81, 85) towards the shoulder, then evenly pick up and k49 (53, 57, 61, 65) (69, 73, 77, 81, 85) towards the underarm, and then finally pick up and k3 (3, 3, 4, 4) (4, 5, 5, 5, 6) from the bind off sts. Place a removable stm in the first st to mark where the mitred decrease will take place [104 (112, 120, 130, 138) (146, 156, 164, 172, 182) sts].

Rounds 1–5: Work in 1x1 ribbing.
Rounds 6–8: Work in 1x1 ribbing until 1 st before center stm, CDD, continue in 1x1 ribbing until end of round [98 (106, 114, 124, 132) (140, 150, 158, 166, 176) sts rem].

Bind off in patt.

FINISHING
Weave in any loose ends. Block your sweater using your preferred method.

JUNIPER VEST CABLE CHARTS AND LEGENDS

Chart A

Legend A

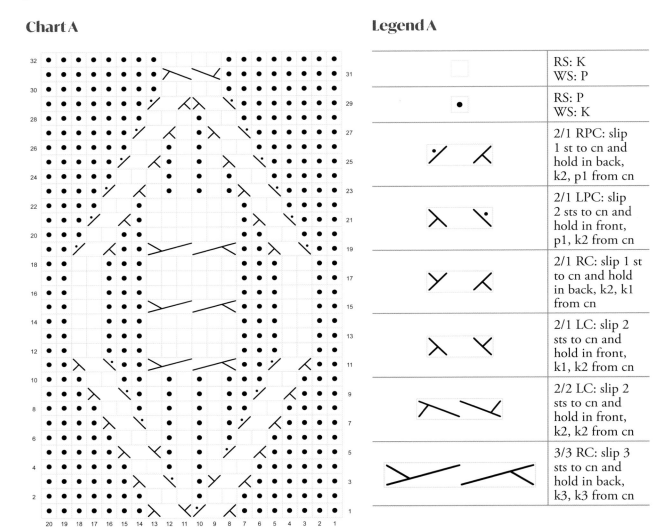

	☐	RS: K WS: P
	•	RS: P WS: K
╱ ╲		2/1 RPC: slip 1 st to cn and hold in back, k2, p1 from cn
╲ ╲		2/1 LPC: slip 2 sts to cn and hold in front, p1, k2 from cn
⋎ ╲		2/1 RC: slip 1 st to cn and hold in back, k2, k1 from cn
⋏ ⋎		2/1 LC: slip 2 sts to cn and hold in front, k1, k2 from cn
⋏╲ ╲		2/2 LC: slip 2 sts to cn and hold in front, k2, k2 from cn
⋎╲ ⋏		3/3 RC: slip 3 sts to cn and hold in back, k3, k3 from cn

Chart B (Right)

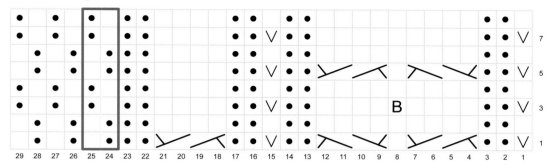

Chart B (Left)

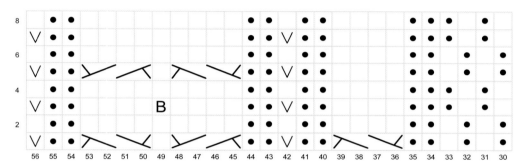

NOTE: Since Chart B is divided in half, this means you will need to read round/row 1 of Chart B (Right) before proceeding to round/row 1 of Chart B (Left).

Legend B

☐	RS: K WS: P
•	RS: P WS: K
V	Sl1wyib
B	MB: (yo, k) 3 times into the next stitch. Turn work. Sl1wyif, p5. Turn work. Sl1wyib, k5. Turn work. (p2tog) 3 times. Turn work. Sl1wyib, k2tog, pass slipped st over the next st [1 st rem]
⟋⟍	2/2 RC: slip 2 sts to cn and hold in back, k2, k2 from cn
⟋⟍	2/2 LC: slip 2 sts to cn and hold in front, k2, k2 from cn
☐	Repeat section 0 (5, 5, 5, 9) (9, 13, 13, 18, 18) more times

OVERSIZED & CHUNKY
Quick Knits that Impress

As soon as the temperature begins to dip, I find myself rummaging through my closet for the coziest sweater I can find. Knitwear is the fashion equivalent of hot chocolate on a wintery day, and you won't be able to convince me otherwise. Slipping on an oversized sweater is an effortless way to look polished yet feel just as comfortable as wearing a pair of sweats. Let's be honest—it's also the more socially acceptable option.

I find myself drawn to chunky knits for so many reasons. Not only are they highly satisfying projects because they knit up quickly, but they are also among the most versatile to style. With no shortage of layering options for added variety and dimension, chunky knits lend themselves well to street-style outfits. In this chapter, you'll find designs that are generously oversized and roomy enough to sneak in a polo shirt, dress or even a thermal layer if you need the extra warmth. Whether you're looking to add a cabled vest or a buttoned jacket to your wardrobe, these bold and functional pieces are the perfect blend of comfort and coziness. Ranging from bulky to super bulky knits, these projects knit up relatively quickly and will keep you feeling toasty all season long.

In this chapter, you'll find bulky weight pullovers like the Fern Pullover (page 57) and the Ginkgo Pullover (page 67). If cardigans are more your cup of tea, the River Birch Jacket (page 73) will make a bold statement in your closet. Last but not least, the small but mighty Morning Glory Vest (page 83) is great for mixing and matching with other pieces.

Fern Pullover

Chunky sweaters are a staple in so many wardrobes, and for good reason. Not only are they fashion forward, but they add comfort, warmth and dimension when paired with a variety of other items in your closet. The Fern Pullover is a chunky cabled crewneck that can be styled in a multitude of ways. Whether worn over a dress shirt for a preppy look or with a pair of mom jeans for a comfy-chic vibe, this sweater is equal parts cozy and versatile. My personal favorite look is wearing the Fern Pullover with a midi-length tulle skirt.

The design features an extra-large moss stitch double diamond cable that is both satisfying and fun to knit. The cable patterns for the body and sleeves are exactly the same, making it easy to memorize and meditative to knit.

Construction Notes

The pullover is worked from the bottom up in the round beginning with a tubular cast on. The body is split and the front and back pieces are knit separately. The shoulders are then seamed and stitches are picked up for the neckband and finished in ribbing. Sleeves are picked up and worked in the round from the top down to the cuffs.

SKILL LEVEL
Intermediate

SIZING
XS (S, M, L, XL) (2XL, 3XL, 4XL, 5XL, 6XL)
42 (46, 50, 54, 58) (62, 66, 70, 74, 78)″ / 106.75 (116.75, 127, 137.25, 147.25) (157.5, 167.75, 177.75, 188, 198) cm, blocked

MATERIALS
Yarn

Bulky weight, Wool and the Gang Alpachino Merino in Cameo Rose (60% Wool, 40% Alpaca), 101 yds (92 m) per 100-g skein

Any bulky weight yarn can be used for this pattern as long as it matches gauge.

Yardage/Meterage

1070 (1175, 1280, 1375, 1480) (1585, 1680, 1785, 1890, 1985) yds / 980 (1075, 1170, 1260, 1355) (1450, 1540, 1635, 1730, 1820) m of bulky weight yarn

Needles

For ribbing: US 8 (5 mm), 24- to 60-inch (60- to 150-cm) circular needles
For body: US 10.5 (6.5 mm), 24- to 60-inch (60- to 150-cm) circular needles
For sleeves: US 8 (5 mm), 16- to 24-inch (40- to 60-cm) circular needles
For cuffs: US 8 (5 mm), double pointed needles

Notions

Cable needle
Crochet hook (optional, for provisional cast on)
Scissors
Scrap yarn
Stitch marker(s)
Tapestry needle

GAUGE

16 sts x 24 rounds = 4 inches (10 cm) in 2x2 ribbing in the round using smaller needles (blocked)

16 sts x 20 rounds = 4 inches (10 cm) in Chart A in the round using larger needles (blocked). You can choose any section of the chart for your gauge swatch.

TECHNIQUES

2x2 Tubular Cast On (explained within the pattern)
Horizontal Invisible Seam (page 161)
Provisional Cast On (page 158)
Kitchener Stitch (page 160)

ABBREVIATIONS

0 or -	no stitch / step does not apply to your size
2x2 ribbing	*k2, p2; repeat from * until end
cn	cable needle
k	knit
k2tog	knit 2 sts together [1 st decreased]
p	purl
p2tog	purl 2 sts together [1 st decreased]
patt	pattern
pm	place marker
rem	remain(ing)
RS	right side
sl1wyib	slip 1 st purlwise with yarn in back
sl2wyib	slip 2 sts purlwise with yarn in back
sl2wyif	slip 2 sts purlwise with yarn in front
ssp	slip 2 sts knitwise, one at a time; move both stitches back to the left needle; purl these 2 sts together through the back loops [1 st decreased]
st(s)	stitch(es)
work(ing) even	continue working the pattern as established without any increases or decreases
WS	wrong side

Cable stitch abbreviations can be found in the Legend on page 63.

SCHEMATIC

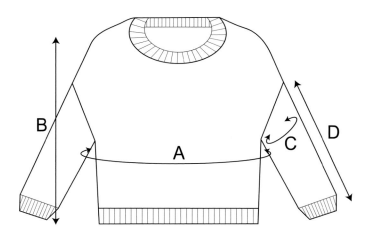

SIZING CHART

		XS	S	M	L	XL	2XL	3XL	4XL	5XL	6XL
A) Body circumference	in	42	46	50	54	58	62	66	70	74	78
	cm	106.75	116.75	127	137.25	147.25	157.5	167.75	177.75	188	198
B) Garment length	in	23	23	23	24	24	25	26	27	27	28
	cm	58.5	58.5	58.5	61	61	63.5	66	68.5	68.5	71
C) Sleeve circumference	in	19	20	21	22	24	24	25	26	27	28
	cm	48.25	50.75	53.25	56	61	61	63.5	66	68.5	71
D) Sleeve length	in	17.5	17.5	18.5	18.5	19.5	19.5	20.5	20.5	20.5	21.5
	cm	44.5	44.5	47	47	49.5	49.5	52	52	52	54.5

This pullover is designed with 12–14 inches (30.5–35.5 cm) of positive ease. Sample shown is knit in size XS.

FERN PULLOVER PATTERN

BODY
2x2 Tubular Cast On

Using US 10.5 (6.5 mm) needles and scrap yarn, cast on 84 (92, 100, 108, 116) (124, 132, 140, 148, 156) sts using the provisional cast on method.

Beginning with the slipknot end, knit 4 rows of stockinette stitch.

Remove the provisional cast on and slip those live sts onto another needle. Line up both needles and fold your work so the RSs are facing out.

Round 1: *K2 from the front needle, p2 from the back needle; repeat from * until end [168 (184, 200, 216, 232) (248, 264, 280, 296, 312) sts]. Pm and join for working in the round.

Switch to US 8 (5 mm) needles and work in 2x2 ribbing for 2.5 inches (6.5 cm).

Switch to US 10.5 (6.5 mm) needles.

Set-up round 1: *P11 (6, 10, 5, 9) (4, 8, 12, 7, 11), work round 1 of Chart A (page 64–65), p11 (6, 10, 5, 9) (4, 8, 12, 7, 11); repeat from * once more.
Set-up round 2: *P11 (6, 10, 5, 9) (4, 8, 12, 7, 11), work round 2 of Chart A, p11 (6, 10, 5, 9) (4, 8, 12, 7, 11); repeat from * once more.

Continue working in patt as established until the piece measures 12.5 (13, 13, 13, 13) (13.5, 13.5, 14, 14, 14) inches / 31.75 (33, 33, 33, 33) (34.25, 34.25, 35.5, 35.5, 35.5) cm from the bottom of the ribbing. Your last round should be an even numbered round.

Separate for Front/Back

Row 1 (RS): P11 (6, 10, 5, 9) (4, 8, 12, 7, 11), work next row of Chart A, p11 (6, 10, 5, 9) (4, 8, 12, 7, 11). Turn work. Leave rem back sts on a holder or spare yarn to return to later.

TIP: Mark where you left off in the chart.

Row 2 (WS): K11 (6, 10, 5, 9) (4, 8, 12, 7, 11), work next row of Chart A, k11 (6, 10, 5, 9) (4, 8, 12, 7, 11).

FRONT RIGHT

Next row (WS): Work in patt.
Next row (RS): Bind off 1 st, work in patt until end.
Repeat the last 2 rows a total of 4 more times [24 (28, 32, 36, 39) (43, 47, 50, 54, 58) sts rem].

Work even until the piece measures 22.5 (22.5, 23, 23.5, 24.25) (25, 25.5, 26.5, 27, 27.5) inches / 57.25 (57.25, 58.5, 59.75, 61.5) (63.5, 64.75, 67.25, 68.5, 69.75) cm from the bottom of the ribbing. Your last row should be a RS row.
Note: Continue working cables even when a portion of the chart has been decreased.

Next row (WS): Bind off 8 (9, 10, 12, 13) (14, 16, 17, 18, 19) sts, work in patt until end [16 (19, 22, 24, 26) (29, 31, 33, 36, 39) sts rem].
Next row (RS): Work in patt.
Next row: Bind off 8 (9, 10, 12, 13) (14, 16, 17, 18, 19) sts, work in patt until end [8 (10, 12, 12, 13) (15, 15, 16, 18, 20) sts rem].
Next row: Work in patt.
Next row: Bind off rem 8 (10, 12, 12, 13) (15, 15, 16, 18, 20) sts.

Break the yarn, leaving a tail that is double the length of the shoulder for seaming.

FRONT LEFT

Rejoin the yarn to WS of work.

Row 1 (WS): Bind off 1 st, work in patt until end.
Row 2 (RS): Work in patt.
Repeat the last 2 rows a total of 4 more times [24 (28, 32, 36, 39) (43, 47, 50, 54, 58) sts rem].

Continue working back and forth in rows in patt until the front piece measures 19 (19, 19.5, 20, 20.75) (21.5, 22, 23, 23.5, 24) inches / 48.25 (48.25, 49.5, 50.75, 52.75) (54.5, 56, 58.5, 59.75, 61) cm from the bottom of the ribbing. Your last row should be a WS row.

Next row (RS): Work 29 (33, 37, 41, 44) (48, 52, 55, 59, 63) sts in patt, bind off 26 (26, 26, 26, 28) (28, 28, 30, 30, 30) sts, work rem 29 (33, 37, 41, 44) (48, 52, 55, 59, 63) sts in patt. Leave front left sts on a holder or spare yarn to return to later.

TIP: Mark where you left off in the chart.

Work even until the piece measures 22.5 (22.5, 23, 23.5, 24.25) (25, 25.5, 26.5, 27, 27.5) inches / 57.25 (57.25, 58.5, 59.75, 61.5) (63.5, 64.75, 67.25, 68.5, 69.75) cm from the bottom of the ribbing. Your last row should be a WS row.

Next row (RS): Bind off 8 (9, 10, 12, 13) (14, 16, 17, 18, 19) sts, work in patt until end [16 (19, 22, 24, 26) (29, 31, 33, 36, 39) sts rem].
Next row (WS): Work in patt.
Next row: Bind off 8 (9, 10, 12, 13) (14, 16, 17, 18, 19) sts, work in patt until end [8 (10, 12, 12, 13) (15, 15, 16, 18, 20) sts rem].
Next row: Work in patt.
Next row: Bind off rem 8 (10, 12, 12, 13) (15, 15, 16, 18, 20) sts.

Break the yarn, leaving a tail that is double the length of the shoulder for seaming.

BACK
Rejoin the yarn to RS of work.

Continue working in patt until the piece measures 22.5 (22.5, 23, 23.5, 24.25) (25, 25.5, 26.5, 27, 27.5) inches / 57.25 (57.25, 58.5, 59.75, 61.5) (63.5, 64.75, 67.25, 68.5, 69.75) cm from the bottom of the ribbing. Your last row should be a WS row.

Next 4 rows: Bind off 8 (9, 10, 12, 13) (14, 16, 17, 18, 19) sts, work in patt until end [52 (56, 60, 60, 64) (68, 68, 72, 76, 80) sts rem].
Next 2 rows: Bind off 8 (10, 12, 12, 13) (15, 15, 16, 18, 20) sts, work in patt until end [36 (36, 36, 36, 38) (38, 38, 40, 40, 40) sts rem].

Bind off rem 36 (36, 36, 36, 38) (38, 38, 40, 40, 40) sts.

NECKBAND
Use the horizontal invisible seaming technique to seam the shoulders.

Using US 8 (5 mm) needles and beginning with the left shoulder, pick up and k15 towards the center front, pick up and k24 (24, 24, 24, 26) (26, 26, 28, 28, 28) from the front bind off sts, pick up and k15 towards right shoulder, and pick up and k34 (34, 34, 34, 36) (36, 36, 38, 38, 38) from the back sts. Pm and join for working in the round [88 (88, 88, 88, 92) (92, 92, 96, 96, 96) sts].

Work in 2x2 ribbing for 1.75 inches (4.5 cm).

Prepare for Tubular Bind Off

Tubular round 1: *K2, sl2wyif; repeat from *
until end.
Tubular round 2: *Sl2wyib, p2; repeat from *
until end.

You will now be rearranging your sts so that all the
knit sts will be slipped to your right-hand needle,
and all the purl sts will be slipped to another needle
and sit at the back.

*Slip the first 2 knit sts to right-hand needle, slip
2 purl sts to back needle; repeat from * until end.

Break the yarn, leaving a tail that is three times
the circumference of the neckline. Bind off using
Kitchener stitch.

SLEEVES (MAKE 2)
Using US 10.5 (6.5 mm) needles and beginning
with the center of the underarm, evenly pick up
and k38 (40, 42, 44, 47) (48, 50, 52, 54, 56)
towards the shoulder, and then evenly pick up and
k38 (40, 42, 44, 47) (48, 50, 52, 54, 56) towards
the underarm. Pm and join for working in the
round [76 (80, 84, 88, 94) (96, 100, 104, 108,
112) sts].

Set-up round 1: P7 (9, 11, 13, 7) (8, 10, 12, 14,
7), work round 1 of Chart A, p7 (9, 11, 13, 7) (8,
10, 12, 14, 7).
Set-up round 2: P7 (9, 11, 13, 7) (8, 10, 12, 14,
7), work round 2 of Chart A, p7 (9, 11, 13, 7) (8,
10, 12, 14, 7).

Continue working the pattern as established until
the sleeve measures 7.5 inches (19 cm) from the
pick up edge.

Decrease round: P1, p2tog, work patt until last 3
sts, ssp, p1 [74 (78, 82, 86, 92) (94, 98, 102, 106,
110) sts rem].

Repeat dec round every 5th (5th, 4th, 3rd, 3rd)
(5th, 4th, 3rd, 4th, 3rd) round 4 (6, 8, 10, 10) (8,
7, 9, 8, 10) more times [66 (66, 66, 66, 72) (78,
84, 84, 90, 90) sts rem].

Work even until the sleeve measures 15 (15, 16,
16, 17) (17, 18, 18, 18, 19) inches / 38 (38, 40.75,
40.75, 43.25) (43.25, 45.75, 45.75, 45.75, 48.25)
cm from the pick up edge, or until it reaches
desired length.

Switch to US 8 (5 mm) needles.

Decrease round: *K1, k2tog; repeat from * until
end [44 (44, 44, 44, 48) (52, 56, 56, 60, 60)
sts rem].

Work in 2x2 ribbing for 2.5 inches (6.5 cm).

Tubular round 1: *K2, sl2wyif; repeat from *
until end.
Tubular round 2: *Sl2wyib, p2; repeat from *
until end.

*Slip the first knit stitches to front needle, slip
2 purl sts to back needle; repeat from * until end.

Break the yarn, leaving a tail that is three times the
circumference of the cuff. Bind off using Kitchener
stitch.

FINISHING
Weave in any loose ends. Block your project using
your preferred method.

LEGEND

☐		RS: K WS: P
•		RS: P WS: K
V		sl1wyib
⟋	⟍	2/1 RPC: slip 1 st to cn and hold in back, k2, p1 from cn
⟍	⟋	2/1 LPC: slip 2 sts to cn and hold in front, p1, k2 from cn
⟋	⟍	2/2 RPC: slip 2 sts to cn and hold in back, k2, p2 from cn
⟍	⟋	2/2 LPC: slip 2 sts to cn and hold in front, p2, k2 from cn
⟋	⟍	2/2 RC: slip 2 sts to cn and hold in back, k2, k2 from cn
⟍	⟋	2/2 LC: slip 2 sts to cn and hold in front, k2, k2 from cn
☐		Body: Repeat section 0 (1, 1, 2, 2) (3, 3, 3, 4, 4) more times. Sleeves: Repeat section 0 (0, 0, 0, 1) (1, 1, 1, 1, 2) more times.

Chart A (Left)

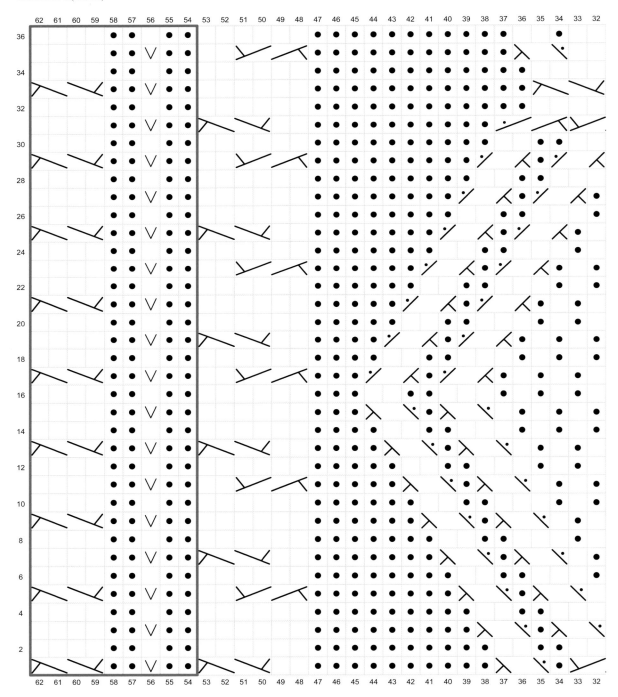

Chart A (Right)

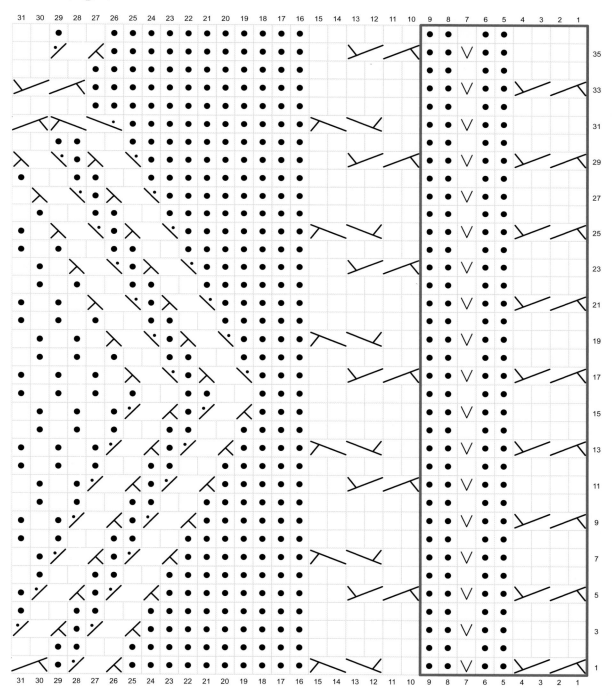

Ginkgo Pullover

Cozy never looked or felt so good. Meet the Ginkgo Pullover, an oversized sweater with no shortage of texture. Chevron cables frame rows of eyelet lace, design elements that are inspired by the ginkgo plant's fan-shaped leaves and plum-like seeds. Wide bubble sleeves give an additional wow factor to this statement piece. Although simple and repetitive to knit, each stitch becomes exaggerated when combined with a super bulky yarn, and the overall result is a striking pattern.

The Ginkgo Pullover is a playful and relaxing knit through and through, and an even more fun piece to wear. Whether layered over a dress, leggings or your go-to denim, the options are endless. Plus, a sweater that can be knit in one weekend is *always* a win in my book.

Construction Notes
The pullover is worked from the bottom up in the round. The front and back pieces are separated and worked flat. The shoulders are seamed using the 3-needle bind off, and stitches are picked up for the neckband. Lastly, stitches are picked up around the armholes and the sleeves are worked from the top down in the round.

SKILL LEVEL
Intermediate

SIZING
XS (S, M, L, XL) (2XL, 3XL, 4XL, 5XL, 6XL)
40.5 (43, 47, 51, 55) (59, 63, 67, 71, 75)" /
102.75 (109.25, 119.5, 129.5, 139.75) (149.75, 160, 170.25, 180.25, 190.5) cm, blocked

MATERIALS
Yarn
Super bulky weight, Stitch & Story The Chunky Wool in Ivory White (100% Merino Wool), 71 yds (65 m) per 100-g skein

Any super bulky weight yarn can be used for this pattern as long as it matches gauge.

Yardage/Meterage
600 (640, 700, 820, 930) (955, 980, 1005, 1065, 1125) yds / 550 (585, 640, 750, 850) (875, 895, 920, 975, 1030) m of super bulky weight yarn

Needles
For ribbing: US 15 (10 mm), 24- to 60-inch (60- to 150-cm) circular needles
For body: US 17 (12 mm), 24- to 60-inch (60- to 150-cm) circular needles
For sleeves: US 17 (12 mm), 16- to 24-inch (40- to 60-cm) circular needles
For cuffs: US 15 (10 mm) double pointed needles

Notions
Cable needle
Scissors
Stitch marker(s)
Tapestry needle

GAUGE
7 sts x 10 rounds = 4 inches (10 cm) in Chart B in the round using larger needles (blocked)

8.5 sts x 14 rounds = 4 inches (10 cm) in moss st in the round using larger needles (blocked)

TECHNIQUES
Longtail Cast On (page 157)
Moss Stitch (page 162)

ABBREVIATIONS

1x1 ribbing	*k1, p1; repeat from * until end
cn	cable needle
k	knit
k2tog	knit two sts together [1 st decreased]
p	purl
patt	pattern
pm	place marker
rem	remain(ing)
RS	right side
st(s)	stitch(es)
work(ing) even	continue working the pattern as established without any increases or decreases
WS	wrong side
yo	yarnover

Cable stitch abbreviations can be found in the Legends on page 72.

SIZING CHART

		XS	S	M	L	XL	2XL	3XL	4XL	5XL	6XL
A) Body circumference	in	40.5	43	47	51	55	59	63	67	71	75
	cm	102.75	109.25	119.5	129.5	139.75	149.75	160	170.25	180.25	190.5
B) Garment length	in	19	19.5	21	21.5	22	23.5	24	24.5	26	26.5
	cm	48.25	49.5	53.25	54.5	56	59.75	61	62.25	66	67.25
C) Sleeve circumference	in	16	17	18	19	20	21	22	23	24	25
	cm	40.75	43.25	45.75	48.25	50.75	53.25	56	58.5	61	63.5
D) Sleeve length	in	15.5	15.5	16	16.5	16.5	17	17.5	17.5	18	18.5
	cm	39.25	39.25	40.75	42	42	43.25	44.5	44.5	45.75	47

This pullover is designed with 9–11 inches (22.75–28 cm) of positive ease. Sample shown is knit in size XS.

SCHEMATIC

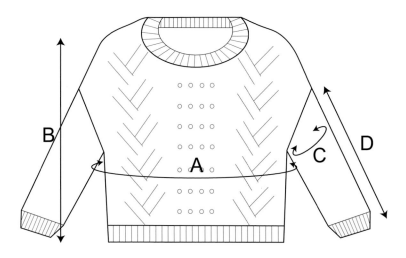

GINGKO PULLOVER PATTERN

BODY

Using US 15 (10 mm) needles, cast on 96 (100, 108, 116, 124) (132, 140, 148, 156, 164) sts using the longtail cast on method. Pm and join for working in the round.

Work in 1x1 ribbing for 2 inches (5 cm).

Switch to US 17 (12 mm) needles.

K 1 round.

Set-up round 1: *Work 6 (6, 8, 8, 10) (12, 14, 16, 16, 18) sts in moss st, work round 1 of Chart A (page 72), work round 1 of Chart B (page 72) over 8 (10, 10, 14, 14) (14, 14, 14, 18, 18) sts, work round 1 of Chart A, work 6 (6, 8, 8, 10) (12, 14, 16, 16, 18) sts in moss st; repeat from * once more.

Set-up round 2: *Work 6 (6, 8, 8, 10) (12, 14, 16, 16, 18) sts in moss st, work round 2 of Chart A, work round 2 of Chart B over 8 (10, 10, 14, 14) (14, 14, 14, 18, 18) sts, work round 2 of Chart A, work 6 (6, 8, 8, 10) (12, 14, 16, 16, 18) sts in moss st; repeat from * once more.

Continue working in patt as established until the piece measures 10 (10, 11, 11, 11) (12, 12, 12, 13, 13) inches / 25.5 (25.5, 28, 28, 28) (30.5, 30.5, 30.5, 33, 33) cm from the cast on edge. Your last round should be an even numbered round.

Separate for Front/Back

Next row (RS): Work 48 (50, 54, 58, 62) (66, 70, 74, 78, 82) sts in patt, turn. Leave rem back sts on a holder or spare yarn to return to later.

TIP: Mark where you left off in the charts.

FRONT RIGHT SHOULDER
Next row (WS): Work in patt.
Next row (RS): Bind off 1 st, work rem sts in patt [19 (20, 22, 24, 25) (27, 29, 30, 32, 34) sts rem]. Repeat the last 2 rows 3 more times until 16 (17, 19, 21, 22) (24, 26, 27, 29, 31) sts rem.

NOTE: Continue working the remaining cables even when part of the chart has been bound off. If you reach a point where there are not enough sts to complete a cable pattern because part of it has been bound off, k the remaining sts instead.

Continue working even until the piece measures 19 (19.5, 21, 21.5, 22) (23.5, 24, 24.5, 26, 26.5) inches / 48.25 (49.5, 53.25, 54.5, 56) (59.75, 61, 62.25, 66, 67.25) cm from the cast on edge. Your last row should be a RS row.

Break the yarn and move live sts to a holder or spare yarn to return to later.

FRONT LEFT SHOULDER
Rejoin the yarn to WS of work.

Next row (WS): Bind off 1 st, work rem sts in patt [19 (20, 22, 24, 25) (27, 29, 30, 32, 34) sts rem].
Next row (RS): Work in patt.
Repeat the last 2 rows 3 more times until 16 (17, 19, 21, 22) (24, 26, 27, 29, 31) sts rem.

Continue working even until the piece measures 19 (19.5, 21, 21.5, 22) (23.5, 24, 24.5, 26, 26.5) inches / 48.25 (49.5, 53.25, 54.5, 56) (59.75, 61, 62.25, 66, 67.25) cm from the cast on edge. Your last row should be a RS row.

Break the yarn and move live sts to a holder or spare yarn to return to later.

FRONT
Next row (WS): Work in patt.

Continue working the front piece in patt until the piece measures 15 (15.5, 17, 17.5, 18) (19.5, 20, 20.5, 22, 22.5) inches / 38 (39.25, 43.25, 44.5, 45.75) (49.5, 50.75, 52, 56, 57.25) cm from the cast on edge. Your last row should be a WS row.

Next row (RS): Work 20 (21, 23, 25, 26) (28, 30, 31, 33, 35) sts in patt, bind off 8 (8, 8, 8, 10) (10, 10, 12, 12, 12) sts, work rem 20 (21, 23, 25, 26) (28, 30, 31, 33, 35) sts in patt. Turn. Leave the front left shoulder sts on the circular needle cord while you work the front right shoulder.

TIP: Mark where you left off in the charts.

BACK
Rejoin the yarn to RS of work.

Work even until the piece measures 17.5 (18, 19.5, 20, 20.5) (22, 22.5, 23, 24.5, 25) inches / 44.5 (45.75, 49.5, 50.75, 52) (56, 57.25, 58.5, 62.25, 63.5) cm from the cast on edge. Your last row should be a WS row.

Next row (RS): Work 18 (19, 21, 23, 24) (26, 28, 29, 31, 33) sts in patt, bind off 12 (12, 12, 12, 14) (14, 14, 16, 16, 16) sts, work rem 18 (19, 21, 23, 24) (26, 28, 29, 31, 33) sts in patt. Leave the back right shoulder sts on the circular needle cord while you work the back left shoulder.

TIP: Mark where you left off in the charts.

BACK LEFT SHOULDER
Next row (WS): Work in patt.
Next row (RS): Bind off 1 st, work rem sts in patt [17 (18, 20, 22, 23) (25, 27, 28, 30, 32) sts rem]. Repeat the last 2 rows 1 more time until 16 (17, 19, 21, 22) (24, 26, 27, 29, 31) sts rem. Flip work so the RSs are facing out and position the left shoulder pieces together. Use the 3-needle bind off method to seam the left shoulder.

BACK RIGHT SHOULDER
Rejoin the yarn to WS of work.

Next row (WS): Bind off 1 st, work in patt until end [17 (18, 20, 22, 23) (25, 27, 28, 30, 32) sts rem].
Next row (RS): Work in patt.
Repeat the last 2 rows 1 more time until 16 (17, 19, 21, 22) (24, 26, 27, 29, 31) sts rem. Flip work so the RSs are facing out and repeat the 3-needle bind off method to seam the right shoulder.

NECKBAND
Flip your work so the RSs are facing out. Using US 15 (10 mm) needles and beginning with the top of the left shoulder, pick up and k9 down the left front, pick up and k8 (8, 8, 8, 10) (10, 10, 12, 12, 12) from the front bind off sts and pick up and k9 up towards the right shoulder. Pick up and k5 towards the center back, pick up and k12 (12, 12, 12, 14) (14, 14, 16, 16, 16) from the back bind off sts, then finally pick up and k5 towards the left shoulder. Pm and join for working in the round [48 (48, 48, 48, 52) (52, 52, 56, 56, 56) sts].

Work in 1x1 ribbing for 1.75 inches (4.5 cm). Bind off loosely in patt.

SLEEVES (MAKE 2)
Using US 17 (12 mm) needles and beginning with the center of the underarm, pick and k20 (21, 23, 24, 25) (26, 27, 28, 29, 30) towards the shoulder, then pick up and k20 (21, 23, 24, 25) (26, 27, 28, 29, 30) back towards the underarm. Pm and join for working in the round [40 (42, 46, 48, 50) (52, 54, 56, 58, 60) sts].

Work in moss st until the sleeve measures 13 (13, 13.5, 14, 14) (14.5, 15, 15, 15.5, 16) inches / 33 (33, 34.25, 35.5, 35.5) (36.75, 38, 38, 39.25, 40.75) cm from the underarm, or until it reaches desired length. Your last round should be an even numbered round.

Switch to US 15 (10 mm) needles.

Sizes XS, L, 2XL, 4XL, 6XL only
Decrease round: *K2tog; repeat from * until end [20 (-, -, 24, -) (26, -, 28, -, 30) sts rem].

Sizes S, M, XL, 3XL, 5XL only
Decrease round: K1, *k2tog; repeat from * until last st, k1 [- (22, 24, -, 26) (-, 28, -, 30, -) sts rem].

All Sizes Resume
Work in 1x1 ribbing for 2 inches (5 cm). Bind off in patt.

FINISHING
Weave in any loose ends. Block your project using your preferred method.

GINKGO PULLOVER CABLE CHARTS AND LEGENDS

Chart A

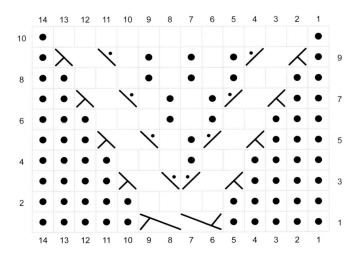

Chart B

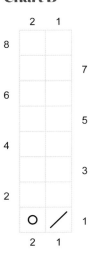

Legend A

☐	RS: K WS: P
•	RS: P WS: K
⟋ ⟍	2/1 RPC: slip 1 st to cn and hold in back, k2, p1 from cn
⟍ ⟋	2/1 LPC: slip 2 sts to cn and hold in front, p1, k2 from cn
⟍⟋	2/2 LC: slip 2 sts to cn and hold in front, k2, k2 from cn

Legend B

☐	RS: K WS: P
⟋	k2tog
○	yo

River Birch Jacket

Transport yourself to the rolling Irish countryside in this modern interpretation of the Aran cardigan. The River Birch Jacket is a chunky and generously oversized garment with room for a sweater underneath. The V-neck and drop shoulders grant the wearer additional fluidity for layering and movement. Designed with comfort and ease of wear in mind, the neckline pairs well with a variety of options underneath: a fitted blouse, a square-neck jumpsuit or a patterned turtleneck just to name a few. The cabled pockets are large enough to store your everyday essentials, or for keeping your hands extra toasty. You'll stay cozy all day in this cocoon of a jacket.

Construction Notes

The jacket is worked from the bottom up in three separate pieces: two front panels and one back piece. The shoulders and sides are seamed, and stitches are picked up around the armholes. The sleeves are then worked from the top down towards the cuff. Stitches are picked up around the front panel edges and the button band is worked in a ribbing before binding off. Optional pockets are knit flat and then seamed to the jacket.

SKILL LEVEL
Intermediate

SIZING
XS (S, M, L, XL) (2XL, 3XL, 4XL, 5XL, 6XL)
40 (48.5, 49.75, 51, 59.5) (60.75, 63.5, 70.5, 71.75, 74.5)" / 101.5 (123.25, 126.25, 129.5, 151.25) (154.25, 161.25, 179, 182.25, 189.25) cm, blocked

MATERIALS
Yarn
Bulky weight, Estelle Yarns Llama Natural Chunky in Cream (80% Merino Wool, 20% Llama), 137 yds (125 m) per 100-g skein

Any bulky weight yarn can be used for this pattern as long as it matches gauge.

Yardage/Meterage
1365 (1610, 1635, 1670, 1910) (1945, 2005, 2215, 2250, 2310) yds / 1250 (1475, 1500, 1530, 1750) (1780, 1835, 2030, 2060, 2115) m of bulky weight yarn

Needles
For ribbing: US 9 (5.5 mm), 24- to 60-inch (60- to 150-cm) circular needles
For body and sleeves: US 10.5 (6.5 mm), 24- to 60-inch (60- to 150-cm) circular needles
For cuffs: US 8 (5 mm) double pointed needles
For button band: US 8 (5 mm), 36- to 60-inch (90- to 150-cm) circular needles

Notions
1" (2.5-cm) buttons (3)
Cable needle
Scissors
Sewing needle and matching thread, fine enough to pass through buttonholes
Scrap yarn in a contrasting color
Stitch markers, ring stitch (1) and locking (3)
Tapestry needle

GAUGE
20 sts x 22 rounds/rows = 4 inches (10 cm) in Chart A worked both flat and in the round using larger needles (blocked)

13 sts x 20 rounds/rows = 4 inches (10 cm) in reverse stockinette worked both flat and in the round using larger needles (blocked)

TECHNIQUES
Horizontal Invisible Seam (page 161)
Longtail Cast On (page 157)
Vertical Invisible Seam (page 161)

ABBREVIATIONS

0 or -	no stitch / step does not apply to your size
1x1 ribbing	*k1, p1; repeat from * until end
cn	cable needle
dec	decrease
k	knit
k2tog	knit 2 sts together [1 st decreased]
p	purl
p2tog	purl 2 sts together [1 st decreased]
patt	pattern
pm	place marker
rem	remain(ing)
RS	right side
sm	slip marker
ssp	slip 2 sts knitwise, one at a time; move both stitches back to the left needle; purl these 2 sts together through the back loops [1 st decreased]
st(s)	stitch(es)
work(ing) even	continue working the pattern as established without any increases or decreases
WS	wrong side

Cable stitch abbreviations can be found in the Legends on pages 80 and 82.

SCHEMATIC

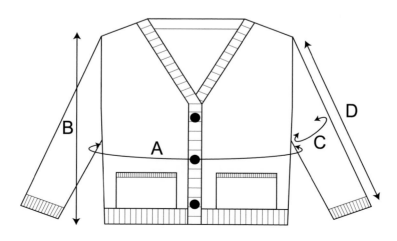

SIZING CHART

		XS	S	M	L	XL	2XL	3XL	4XL	5XL	6XL
A) Body circumference (buttoned)	in	40	48.5	49.75	51	59.5	60.75	63.5	70.5	71.75	74.5
	cm	101.5	123.25	126.25	129.5	151.25	154.25	161.25	179	182.25	189.25
B) Garment length	in	23	23	23.5	23.5	24	24	24.5	24.5	25	25.5
	cm	58.5	58.5	59.75	59.75	61	61	62.25	62.25	63.5	64.75
C) Sleeve circumference	in	14.25	15	15.75	16.25	19.25	19.75	20.5	21.75	24.75	25.25
	cm	36.25	38	40	41.25	49	50.25	52	55.25	62.75	64.25
D) Sleeve length	in	16.5	16.5	17	17	17.5	17.5	18	18	18.5	18.5
	cm	42	42	43.25	43.25	44.5	44.5	45.75	45.75	47	47

This jacket is designed with 9–16 inches (22.75–40.75 cm) of positive ease. Sample shown is knit in size XS.

RIVER BIRCH JACKET PATTERN

RIGHT FRONT

Using US 9 (5.5 mm) needles, cast on 46 (54, 55, 56, 64) (65, 67, 74, 75, 77) sts using the longtail cast on method.

Work in 1x1 ribbing for 10 rows.

Switch to US 10.5 (6.5 mm) needles. P one row.

Set-up row 1 (RS): P2, work row 1 of Chart A (page 81), work row 1 of Chart B (page 82) 0 (1, 1, 1, 2) (2, 2, 3, 3, 3) times, p4 (2, 3, 4, 2) (3, 5, 2, 3, 5).

Set-up row 2 (WS): K4 (2, 3, 4, 2) (3, 5, 2, 3, 5), work row 2 of Chart B 0 (1, 1, 1, 2) (2, 2, 3, 3, 3) times, work row 2 of Chart A, k2.

Continue working patt as established until the piece measures 11.5 (11.5, 12, 12, 12.5) (12.5, 13, 13, 13.5, 14) inches / 29.25 (29.25, 30.5, 30.5, 31.75) (31.75, 33, 33, 34.25, 35.5) cm from the cast on edge. Your last row should be a WS row.

TIP: Mark where you left off in the charts.

Begin Decreases

Row 1 (RS, decrease): Bind off 1 st, work in patt until end [45 (53, 54, 55, 63) (64, 66, 73, 74, 76) sts rem].
Row 2 (WS): Work in patt.
Repeat the last 2 rows 20 more times until 25 (33, 34, 35, 43) (44, 46, 53, 54, 56) sts rem.

Repeat dec row [24 (32, 33, 34, 42) (43, 45, 52, 53, 55) sts rem].

Work three rows even.

Repeat dec row [23 (31, 32, 33, 41) (42, 44, 51, 52, 54) sts rem].

Work even until the piece measures 23 (23, 23.5, 23.5, 24) (24, 24.5, 24.5, 25, 25.5) inches / 58.5 (58.5, 59.75, 59.75, 61) (61, 62.25, 62.25, 63.5, 64.75) cm from the cast on edge. Your last row should be a RS row.

TIP: Mark where you left off in the charts.

Next row (WS): Bind off 8 (10, 11, 11, 14) (14, 15, 17, 17, 18) sts, work in patt until end [15 (21, 21, 22, 27) (28, 29, 34, 35, 36) sts rem].
Next row (RS): Work in patt.
Next row: Bind off 8 (10, 11, 11, 14) (14, 15, 17, 17, 18) sts, work in patt until end [7 (11, 10, 11, 13) (14, 14, 17, 18, 18) sts rem].
Next row: Work in patt.
Next row: Bind off rem 7 (11, 10, 11, 13) (14, 14, 17, 18, 18) sts.

Break the yarn, leaving a tail that is double the length of the shoulder for seaming.

LEFT FRONT
Using US 9 (5.5 mm) needles, cast on 46 (54, 55, 56, 64) (65, 67, 74, 75, 77) sts using the longtail cast on method.

Work in 1x1 ribbing for ten rows.

Switch to US 10.5 (6.5 mm) needles. P one row.

Set-up row 1 (RS): P4 (2, 3, 4, 2) (3, 5, 2, 3, 5), work row 1 of Chart B 0 (1, 1, 1, 2) (2, 2, 3, 3, 3) times, work row 1 of Chart A, p2.
Set-up row 2 (WS): K2, work row 2 of Chart A, work row 2 of Chart B 0 (1, 1, 1, 2) (2, 2, 3, 3, 3) times, k4 (2, 3, 4, 2) (3, 5, 2, 3, 5).

Continue working patt as established until the piece measures 11.5 (11.5, 12, 12, 12.5) (12.5, 13, 13, 13.5, 14) inches / 29.25 (29.25, 30.5, 30.5, 31.75) (31.75, 33, 33, 34.25, 35.5) cm from the cast on edge. Your last row should be a WS row.

> **TIP:** Make sure this matches where you left off on the front right piece.

Begin Decreases
Row 1 (RS): Work in patt.
Row 2 (WS, Decrease): Bind off 1 st, work in patt until end [45 (53, 54, 55, 63) (64, 66, 73, 74, 76) sts rem].

Repeat the last 2 rows 21 more times until 24 (32, 33, 34, 42) (43, 45, 52, 53, 55) sts rem.

Work 3 rows even.

Repeat dec row [23 (31, 32, 33, 41) (42, 44, 51, 52, 54) sts rem].

Work even until the piece measures 23 (23, 23.5, 23.5, 24) (24, 24.5, 24.5, 25, 25.5) inches / 58.5 (58.5, 59.75, 59.75, 61) (61, 62.25, 62.25, 63.5, 64.75) cm from the cast on edge. Your last row should be a WS row.

Next row (RS): Bind off 8 (10, 11, 11, 14) (14, 15, 17, 17, 18) sts, work in patt until end [15 (21, 21, 22, 27) (28, 29, 34, 35, 36) sts rem].
Next row (WS): Work in patt.
Next row: Bind off 8 (10, 11, 11, 14) (14, 15, 17, 17, 18) sts, work in patt until end [7 (11, 10, 11, 13) (14, 14, 17, 18, 18) sts rem].

Set-up row 1 (RS): P4 (2, 3, 4, 2) (3, 5, 2, 3, 5), work row 1 of Chart B 0 (1, 1, 1, 2) (2, 2, 3, 3, 3) times, work row 1 of Chart A, work row 1 of Chart B, work row 1 of Chart A, work row 1 of Chart B 0 (1, 1, 1, 2) (2, 2, 3, 3, 3) times, p4 (2, 3, 4, 2) (3, 5, 2, 3, 5).

Set-up row 2 (WS): K4 (2, 3, 4, 2) (3, 5, 2, 3, 5), work row 2 of Chart B 0 (1, 1, 1, 2) (2, 2, 3, 3, 3) times, work row 2 of Chart A, work row 2 of Chart B, work row 2 of Chart A, work row 2 of Chart B 0 (1, 1, 1, 2) (2, 2, 3, 3, 3) times, k4 (2, 3, 4, 2) (3, 5, 2, 3, 5).

Work even until the piece matches the point in which the shoulder bind offs begin on the front panels [approximately 23 (23, 23.5, 23.5, 24) (24, 24.5, 24.5, 25, 25.5) inches / 58.5 (58.5, 59.75, 59.75, 61) (61, 62.25, 62.25, 63.5, 64.75) cm from the cast on edge]. Your last row should be a WS row.

Next 2 rows: Bind off 8 (10, 11, 11, 14) (14, 15, 17, 17, 18) sts, work in patt until end [82 (94, 94, 96, 106) (108, 110, 120, 122, 124) sts rem].
Next 2 rows: Bind off 8 (10, 11, 11, 14) (14, 15, 17, 17, 18) sts, work in patt until end [66 (74, 72, 74, 78) (80, 80, 86, 88, 88) sts rem].
Next 2 rows: Bind off 7 (11, 10, 11, 13) (14, 14, 17, 18, 18) sts, work in patt until end [52 for all sizes sts rem].

Bind off rem 52 sts for all sizes.

Position the front and back pieces with the RSs facing out. Using a tapestry needle, seam the shoulders using the horizontal invisible seaming technique. Seam the sides from the cast on edge towards the shoulders using the vertical invisible seaming technique, leaving a 9 (9.5, 10, 10.5, 11) (11.5, 12, 12.5, 13, 13.5) inch / 22.75 (24.25, 25.5, 26.75, 28) (29.25, 30.5, 31.75, 33, 34.25) cm opening for the sleeves.

Next row: Work in patt.
Next row: Bind off rem 7 (11, 10, 11, 13) (14, 14, 17, 18, 18) sts.

Break the yarn, leaving a tail that is double the length of the shoulder for seaming.

BACK
Using US 9 (5.5 mm) needles, cast on 98 (114, 116, 118, 134) (136, 140, 154, 156, 160) sts using the longtail cast on method.

Work in 1x1 ribbing for 10 rows.

Switch to US 10.5 (6.5 mm) needles. P one row.

SLEEVES (MAKE 2)

Using US 10.5 (6.5 mm) needles and beginning with the center of the underarm, evenly pick up and k32 (33, 34, 35, 41) (42, 43, 45, 51, 52) towards the shoulder, then evenly pick up and k32 (33, 34, 35, 41) (42, 43, 45, 51, 52) back towards the underarm. Pm and join for working in the round [64 (66, 68, 70, 82) (84, 86, 90, 102, 104) sts].

Set-up round 1: P2 (3, 4, 5, 1) (2, 3, 5, 1, 2), work round 1 of Chart B 1 (1, 1, 1, 2) (2, 2, 2, 3, 3) times, work round 1 of Chart A, work round 1 of Chart B 1 (1, 1, 1, 2) (2, 2, 2, 3, 3) times, p2 (3, 4, 5, 1) (2, 3, 5, 1, 2).

Set-up round 2: P2 (3, 4, 5, 1) (2, 3, 5, 1, 2), work round 2 of Chart B 1 (1, 1, 1, 2) (2, 2, 2, 3, 3) times, work round 2 of Chart A, work round 2 of Chart B 1 (1, 1, 1, 2) (2, 2, 2, 3, 3) times, p2 (3, 4, 5, 1) (2, 3, 5, 1, 2).

Continue working patt as established until the sleeve measures 8.5 (8.5, 8.5, 8.5, 7) (7.5, 7.5, 7, 6.5, 6.5) inches / 21.5 (21.5, 21.5, 21.5, 17.75) (19, 19, 17.75, 16.5, 16.5) cm from the pick up edge.

Decrease round: P1, p2tog, work in patt until last 3 sts, ssp, p1 [62 (64, 66, 68, 80) (82, 84, 88, 100, 102) sts rem].

Repeat dec round every 6th (6th, 6th, 6th, 4th) (5th, 5th, 5th, 4th, 4th) round 3 (4, 5, 6, 12) (9, 10, 12, 14, 15) more times [56 (56, 56, 56, 56) (64, 64, 64, 72, 72) sts rem].

Work even until the sleeve measures 14.5 (14.5, 15, 15, 15.5) (15.5, 16, 16, 16.5, 16.5) inches / 36.75 (36.75, 38, 38, 39.25) (39.25, 40.75, 40.75, 42, 42) cm from the pick up edge, or until it reaches desired length.

Switch to US 8 (5 mm) needles.

Next round: *K2, k2tog; repeat from * until end [42 (42, 42, 42, 42) (48, 48, 48, 54, 54) sts rem].

Work in 1x1 ribbing for 10 rounds. Bind off in patt.

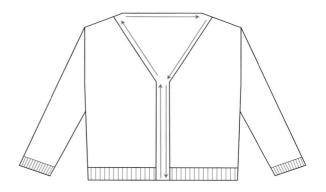

BUTTON BAND

Using US 8 (5 mm) needles and beginning with the cast on edge of the front right panel, pick up and knit 3 sts out of every 4 rows up towards the back neck, evenly pick up and k42 (44, 44, 42, 44) (42, 42, 44, 42, 42) sts along the back neck, then pick up and knit 3 sts for every 4 rows along left front to lower edge.

Row 1 (WS): *P1, k1; rep from * to last st, p1.
Row 2 (RS): *K1, p1; rep from * to last st, k1.
Row 3: Repeat row 1.

Place 3 removable markers along the right front, with the topmost being at the beginning of the V-neck shaping, the bottommost about an inch (2.5 cm) from the bottom hem, and one spaced evenly between.

Row 4: *Work in established ribbing to first marker, sm, bind off 2 sts; rep from * 2 more times, work in established ribbing until end.
Row 5: *Work in established ribbing to first marker, cast on 2 sts, remove marker; rep from * 2 more times, work in established ribbing until end.
Rows 6–9: Work in established ribbing until end.

Bind off knitwise. Sew the buttons to left front opposite the buttonholes.

POCKETS (OPTIONAL—MAKE 2)

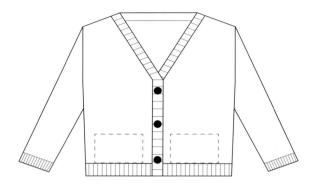

Using US 10.5 (6.5 mm) needles, cast on 40 sts using the longtail cast on method.

Next row (WS): P one row.

Work rows 1–16 of Chart A, and then rows 1–9 once more.

Next row (WS): P one row.

Switch to US 8 (5 mm) needles.

Work in 1x1 ribbing for 4 rows. Bind off knitwise.

Using a contrasting piece of scrap yarn, mark the pocket placements. The pockets are placed immediately above the bottom ribbing. Ensure the cable patterns from the pocket and the front panel are aligned. Use the vertical invisible seaming technique to seam the sides of the pockets to the front panels, and the horizontal invisible seaming technique to seam the bottom. Weave in any loose ends and remove the scrap yarn.

FINISHING

Weave in any loose ends. Block your project using your preferred method.

RIVER BIRCH JACKET CABLE CHARTS AND LEGENDS

Legend A

	RS: K WS: P
•	RS: P WS: K
⟋ ⟍	2/1 RPC: slip 1 st to cn and hold in back, k2, p1 from cn
⟍ ⟋	2/1 LPC: slip 2 sts to cn and hold in front, p1, k2 from cn
⟍⟋	2/2 RC: slip 2 sts to cn and hold in back, k2, k2 from cn
⟋⟍	2/2 LC: slip 2 sts to cn and hold in front, k2, k2 from cn
⟍	2/2 RPC: slip 2 sts to cn and hold in back, k2, p2 from cn
⟋	2/2 LPC: slip 2 sts to cn and hold in front, p2, k2 from cn

NOTE: Since Chart A is divided in half, this means you will need to read round/row 1 of Chart A (Right) before proceeding to round/row 1 of Chart A (Left).

Chart A (Right)

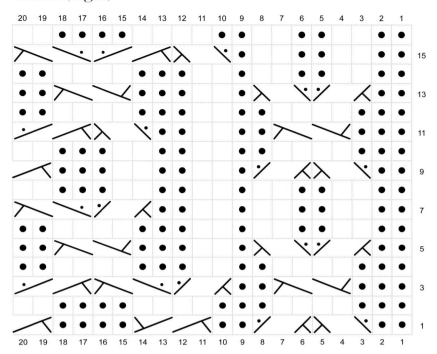

Chart A (Left)

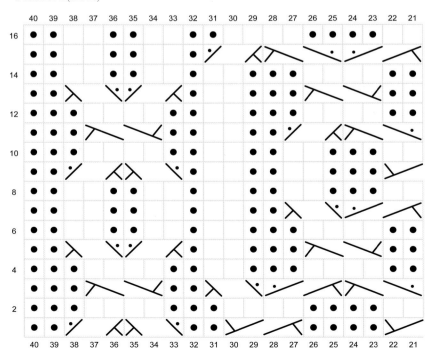

Chart B

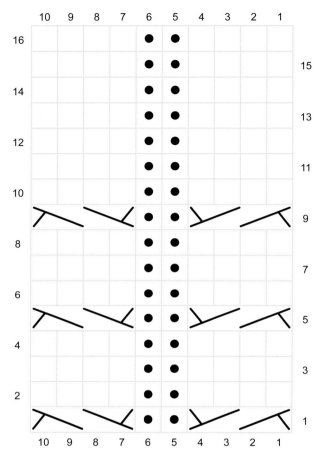

Legend B

☐	RS: K WS: P
•	RS: P WS: K
⟍⟋	2/2 RC: slip 2 sts to cn and hold in back, k2, k2 from cn
⟋⟍	2/2 LC: slip 2 sts to cn and hold in front, k2, k2 from cn

Morning Glory Vest

The Morning Glory Vest is a small garment with a big personality. Ultra-cropped and chunky with a versatile crew neck, this vest is oh-so-cute not only as a standalone garment but also as a transitional layering piece. Slip it over a crisp white T-shirt for a simple and casual outfit, or layer it over a fitted top with statement sleeves if you're feeling fancy. Like the morning glory flower, this project will bloom before your eyes and fly off the needles. The ribbing is knit in a contrasting color for added dimension, but the vest can also be knit in one single color if that's your preference!

Construction Notes

The vest is worked from the bottom up in the round, beginning with a ribbing knit with the contrast color yarn before switching to the main color for the body. The piece is then separated at the armholes and the front and back pieces are knit flat. The front and back pieces are seamed together using the 3-needle bind off. Using the contrast color once again, stitches are picked up for both the armhole and neck edges and finished with ribbing.

SKILL LEVEL
Advanced Beginner

SIZING
XS (S, M, L, XL) (2XL, 3XL, 4XL, 5XL, 6XL)
30 (34, 38, 42, 46) (50.75, 54.75, 58.75, 62.75, 66.75)″ / 76.25 (86.25, 96.5, 106.75, 116.75) (129, 139, 149.25, 159.5, 169.5) cm, blocked

MATERIALS
Yarn

MC: Super bulky weight, Stitch & Story The Chunky Wool in Iced Mint (100% Merino Wool), 71 yds (65 m) per 100-g skein

CC: Super bulky weight, Stitch & Story The Chunky Wool in Ivory White (100% Merino Wool), 71 yds (65 m) per 100-g skein

Any super bulky weight yarn can be used for this pattern as long as it matches gauge.

Yardage/Meterage
150 (180, 200, 215, 235) (275, 290, 315, 325, 335) yds / 135 (165, 185, 195, 215) (250, 265, 285, 295, 305) m of super bulky weight yarn in main color (MC)
and
60 (75, 85, 90, 100) (110, 120, 130, 140, 150) yds / 55 (65, 75, 80, 90) (100, 110, 115, 125, 135) m of super bulky weight yarn in contrast color (CC)

Needles
For ribbing: US 13 (9 mm), 24- to 60-inch (60- to 150-cm) circular needles
For body: US 17 (12 mm), 24- to 60-inch (60- to 150-cm) circular needles

Notions
Cable needle
Scrap yarn or stitch holder
Scissors
Stitch markers
Tapestry needle

GAUGE
8 sts x 12 rounds = 4 inches (10 cm) in moss st worked in the round using larger needles (blocked)

10 sts x 10 rounds = 4 inches (10 cm) in Chart A worked in the round using larger needles (blocked)

TECHNIQUES
3-Needle Bind Off (page 159)
Longtail Cast On (page 157)
Moss Stitch (page 162)

ABBREVIATIONS

0 or -	no stitch / step does not apply to your size
1x1 ribbing	*k1, p1; repeat from * repeat until end
CC	contrast color
cn	cable needle
k	knit
MC	main color
p	purl
patt	pattern
pm	place marker
rem	remain(ing)
RS	right side
sm	slip marker
st(s)	stitch(es)
stm	stitch marker
work(ing) even	continue working the pattern as established without any increases or decreases
WS	wrong side

Cable stitch abbreviations can be found in the Legends on page 89.

SCHEMATIC

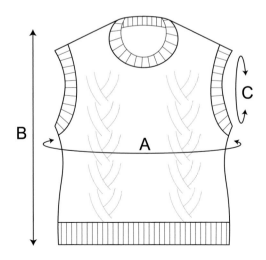

SIZING CHART

		XS	S	M	L	XL	2XL	3XL	4XL	5XL	6XL
A) Body circumference	in	30	34	38	42	46	50.75	54.75	58.75	62.75	66.75
	cm	76.25	86.25	96.5	106.75	116.75	129	139	149.25	159.5	169.5
B) Garment length	in	15	16	17	17.5	18.5	19.5	20	21	22	23.5
	cm	38	40.75	43.25	44.5	47	49.5	50.75	53.25	56	59.75
C) Armhole circumference	in	16	17	18	19	20	21	22	23	24	25
	cm	40.75	43.25	45.75	48.25	50.75	53.25	56	58.5	61	63.5

This vest is designed with 0–2 inches (0–5 cm) of positive ease. If in between sizes, the smaller size is recommended. Sample shown is knit in size XS.

MORNING GLORY VEST PATTERN

BODY
Using US 13 (9 mm) needles and CC, cast on 72 (80, 88, 96, 104) (116, 124, 132, 140, 148) sts using the longtail cast on method. Pm and join for working in the round.

Work in 1x1 ribbing for 8 (8, 8, 8, 8) (10, 10, 10, 10, 10) rounds.

Next row: K all.

Switch to US 17 (12 mm) needles and MC.

Set-up round 1: *Work 4 (4, 6, 6, 8) (8, 10, 10, 12, 12) sts in moss st, p2, work row 1 of Chart A (page 89), p2, work 8 (12, 12, 16, 16) (14, 14, 18, 18, 22) sts in moss st, p2, work row 1 of Chart A, p2, work 4 (4, 6, 6, 8) (8, 10, 10, 12, 12) sts in moss st; pm for side and repeat from * once more.
Set-up round 2: *Work 4 (4, 6, 6, 8) (8, 10, 10, 12, 12) sts in moss st, p2, work row 2 of Chart A, p2, work 8 (12, 12, 16, 16) (14, 14, 18, 18, 22) sts in moss st, p2, work row 2 of Chart A, p2, work 4 (4, 6, 6, 8) (8, 10, 10, 12, 12) sts in moss st; sm and repeat from * once more.

Continue working patt as established until the piece measures 7 (7.5, 8, 8, 8.5) (9, 9, 9.5, 10, 11) inches / 17.75 (19, 20.25, 20.25, 21.5) (22.75, 22.75, 24.25, 25.5, 28) cm from the cast on edge. Your last round should be an even numbered round.

NOTE: This vest is very cropped. If you want to add additional length to the garment, do so here. Ensure you add the same amount to all other sections related to the body wherever a length is provided.

Separate for Front/Back
Next row (RS): Bind off 2 (2, 2, 2, 2) (3, 3, 3, 3, 3) sts, work in patt until side stm. Remove side marker and turn. Leave rem back sts on a holder or spare yarn to return to later [34 (38, 42, 46, 50) (55, 59, 63, 67, 71) sts rem].

TIP: Mark where you left off in the chart.

FRONT
Next row (WS): Bind off 2 (2, 2, 2, 2) (3, 3, 3, 3, 3) sts, work in patt until end [32 (36, 40, 44, 48) (52, 56, 60, 64, 68) sts rem].
Next row (RS): Bind off 1 st, work in patt until end [31 (35, 39, 43, 47) (51, 55, 59, 63, 67) sts rem].

Next row (WS): Bind off 1 st, work in patt until end [30 (34, 38, 42, 46) (50, 54, 58, 62, 66) sts rem].
Repeat the last 2 rows 1 more time [28 (32, 36, 40, 44) (48, 52, 56, 60, 64) sts rem].

Continue working patt as established until the piece measures 10 (10.5, 11, 11, 11.5) (12, 12, 12.5, 13, 14) inches / 25.5 (26.75, 28, 28, 29.25) (30.5, 30.5, 31.75, 33, 35.5) cm from the cast on edge. Your last row should be a WS row.

Next row (RS): Work 12 (14, 16, 18, 20) (22, 24, 26, 28, 30) sts in patt, bind off 4 sts, work rem 12 (14, 16, 18, 20) (22, 24, 26, 28, 30) sts in patt. Set aside front left sts on a holder or spare yarn to return to later.

TIP: Mark where you left off in the chart.

FRONT RIGHT
Next row (WS): Work in patt.
Next row (RS): Bind off 1 st, work in patt until end [11 (13, 15, 17, 19) (21, 23, 25, 27, 29) sts rem].
Repeat the last 2 rows 1 more time [10 (12, 14, 16, 18) (20, 22, 24, 26, 28) sts rem].

Work even until the front right measures 15 (16, 17, 17.5, 18.5) (19.5, 20, 21, 22, 23.5) inches / 38 (40.75, 43.25, 44.5, 47) (49.5, 50.75, 53.25, 56, 59.75) cm from the cast on edge. Your last row should be a WS row. Break the yarn and move live sts to a holder or spare yarn to return to later.

FRONT LEFT
Rejoin the yarn to WS of work.

Next row (WS): Bind off 1 st, work in patt until end [11 (13, 15, 17, 19) (21, 23, 25, 27, 29) sts rem].
Next row (RS): Work in patt.
Repeat the last 2 rows 1 more time [10 (12, 14, 16, 18) (20, 22, 24, 26, 28) sts rem].

Work even until the front right measures 15 (16, 17, 17.5, 18.5) (19.5, 20, 21, 22, 23.5) inches / 38 (40.75, 43.25, 44.5, 47) (49.5, 50.75, 53.25, 56, 59.75) cm from the cast on edge. Your last row should be a WS row. Break the yarn and move live sts to a holder or spare yarn to return to later.

BACK
Rejoin the yarn to RS of work.

Row 1 (RS): Bind off 2 (2, 2, 2, 2) (3, 3, 3, 3, 3) sts, work in patt until end [34 (38, 42, 46, 50) (55, 59, 63, 67, 71) sts rem].
Row 2 (WS): Bind off 2 (2, 2, 2, 2) (3, 3, 3, 3, 3) sts, work in patt until end [32 (36, 40, 44, 48) (52, 56, 60, 64, 68) sts rem].

Row 3: Bind off 1 st, work in patt until end [31 (35, 39, 43, 47) (51, 55, 59, 63, 67) sts rem].
Row 4: Bind off 1 st, work in patt until end [30 (34, 38, 42, 46) (50, 54, 58, 62, 66) sts rem]. Repeat rows 3 and 4 one more time [28 (32, 36, 40, 44) (48, 52, 56, 60, 64) sts rem].

Work even until the back piece measures 15 (16, 17, 17.5, 18.5) (19.5, 20, 21, 22, 23.5) inches / 38 (40.75, 43.25, 44.5, 47) (49.5, 50.75, 53.25, 56, 59.75) cm from the cast on edge. Your last row should be a WS row.

Do not break the yarn. Move the front right sts to another needle. Arrange the back and front right pieces so the RSs are facing each other. Use the 3-needle bind off method to attach the left shoulder to the back piece. Continue binding off the back neck sts until 10 (12, 14, 16, 18) (20, 22, 24, 26, 28) sts rem, then use the 3-needle bind off to attach the right shoulder sts to the remaining back sts.

ARMHOLE EDGE (MAKE 2)
Flip work so the RSs are facing out. Using US 13 (9 mm) needles and CC and beginning with the center of the underarm, pick up and k2 (2, 2, 2, 2) (3, 3, 3, 3, 3) from the bind off edge, evenly pick up and k22 (23, 25, 26, 27) (28, 30, 31, 32, 33) towards the shoulder, evenly pick up and k22 (23, 25, 26, 27) (28, 30, 31, 32, 33) back towards the underarm, then pick up and k2 (2, 2, 2, 2) (3, 3, 3, 3, 3) from the bind off edge. Pm and join for working in the round [48 (50, 54, 56, 58) (62, 66, 68, 70, 72) sts].

Work in 1x1 ribbing for 2 rounds. Bind off in patt.

NECKBAND
Using US 13 (9 mm) needles and CC and beginning at the left shoulder seam, evenly pick up and k16 (17, 18, 18, 19) (19, 20, 20, 21, 22) down the neck edge, pick up and k4 from the front bind off edge, evenly pick up and k16 (17, 18, 18, 19) (19, 20, 20, 21, 22) up towards the right shoulder, and evenly pick up and k12 from the back piece. Pm and join for working in the round [48 (50, 52, 52, 54) (54, 56, 56, 58, 60) sts].

Work in 1x1 ribbing for 2 rounds. Bind off loosely in patt.

FINISHING
Weave in any loose ends. Block your project using your preferred method.

MORNING GLORY VEST CABLE CHARTS AND LEGENDS

Chart A Sizes XS–XL

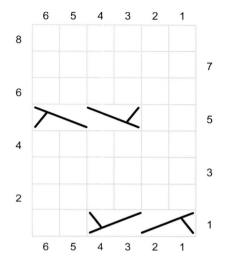

Chart A Sizes 2XL–6XL

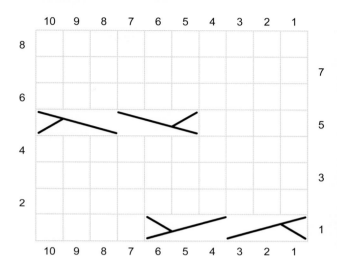

Legend A Sizes XS–XL

	RS: K WS: P
⧄	2/2 RC: slip 2 sts to cn and hold in back, k2, k2 from cn
⧅	2/2 LC: slip 2 sts to cn and hold in front, k2, k2 from cn

Legend A Sizes 2XL–6XL

	RS: K WS: P
⧄	3/3 RC: slip 3 sts to cn and hold in back, k3, k3 from cn
⧅	3/3 LC: slip 3 sts to cn and hold in front, k3, k3 from cn

Simple & Clean

Subtle & Uncomplicated Cables

When it comes to cable sweaters, you may think of intricate twists, braids and lattices from top to bottom. However, cable garments don't necessarily have to be complicated. In fact, sometimes less is more! With that in mind, I wanted to dedicate a section of this book to garments that are an ode to simplicity. While these designs may be more minimalist in style, they are far from monotonous.

The designs in this chapter feature cable work alongside basic stitches, resulting in subtle and refined garments with a modern sensibility. The yarns used in these designs were purposefully chosen to create the perfect amount of drape, density and texture to complement the cables. The result? Three closet staples that are feminine in an understated way. The simple winding cables of the Willow Pullover (page 101) evoke a romantic sentiment, while the side cables of the Mulberry Poncho (page 93) will keep you looking polished regardless of the layer underneath. Last but not least, the Sagebrush Sweater (page 109) is the perfect blend of casual and sophisticated, the cabled yoke an elegant contrast to its sweatshirt-style silhouette. No matter the occasion, these pieces will be cozy and timeless additions to your handknit wardrobe.

Mulberry Poncho

A knit poncho is one of the most versatile outerwear pieces in any wardrobe. After all, what's better than a wearable blanket? A wearable blanket that you hand knit yourself, of course. The Mulberry Poncho is an elegant garment that features a symmetrical cable pattern down the sides. Knit with a blown alpaca yarn for the ultimate drape and softness, the result is a warm but airy fabric with a hint of fuzz.

The poncho is a comfortable and cozy garment that is stylish and easy to layer: The sides can be buttoned to create large arm openings, or the poncho can be worn completely open over another knit sweater. Either way, the ribbed turtleneck will keep you feeling snug regardless of how you choose to style your outfit. In cooler weather, slip the poncho on to elevate a pair of tapered pants, leather leggings or even a skintight jumpsuit. Complete your outfit with a pair of booties or knee-highs for a chic ensemble.

Construction Notes
The poncho is worked flat in two panels from the bottom up. The button band is knit alongside both front and back panels, with the buttonholes worked into the back panel only. The front and back panels have simple neck shaping, and once both panels are completed, the shoulders are joined using the 3-needle bind off. Stitches are picked up around the neckline for the turtleneck. The buttons are hand sewn to the front panel to correspond to the buttonholes on the back panel.

SKILL LEVEL
Intermediate

SIZING
XS/S (M/L, XL/2XL, 3XL/4XL, 5XL/6XL)
56.25 (64.25, 72.25, 80.75, 88)" / 143 (163.25, 183.5, 205, 223.5) cm, blocked

MATERIALS
Yarn
Aran weight, Estelle Yarns Alpaca Drift in Birch (70% Baby Alpaca, 7% Merino Wool, 23% Nylon), 142 yds (130 m) per 50-g skein

Any Aran weight yarn can be used for this pattern as long as it matches gauge.

Yardage/Meterage
1420 (1530, 1585, 1775, 1905) yds / 1300 (1400, 1450, 1625, 1745) m of Aran weight yarn

Needles
For ribbing: US 8 (5 mm), 24- to 60-inch (60- to 150-cm) circular needles
For body: US 9 (5.5 mm), 24- to 60-inch (60- to 150-cm) circular needles

Notions
1" (2.5-cm) buttons (4)
Cable needle
Scissors
Scrap yarn or stitch holder
Sewing needle and matching thread
Stitch markers, ring stitch (4) and locking (4)
Tapestry needle

GAUGE
20 sts x 23 rows = 4 inches (10 cm) in stockinette st worked flat using larger needles (blocked)

28 sts x 25 rows = 4 inches (10 cm) in Chart A worked flat using larger needles (blocked)

TECHNIQUES
3-Needle Bind Off (page 159)
Longtail Cast On (page 157)

ABBREVIATIONS

2x2 ribbing	*k2, p2; repeat from * until end
cn	cable needle
k	knit
k2tog	knit 2 sts together [1 st decreased]
p	purl
patt	pattern
pm	place marker
rem	remain(ing)
RS	right side
sl1wyib	slip 1 st purlwise with yarn in back
sm	slip marker
ssk	slip 2 sts knitwise, one at a time; move both stitches back to the left needle; knit these 2 sts together through the back loops [1 st decreased]
st(s)	stitch(es)
stm(s)	stitch marker(s)
work(ing) even	continue working the pattern as established without any increases or decreases
WS	wrong side
yo	yarnover

Cable stitch abbreviations can be found in the Legends on pages 98–99.

SIZING CHART

		XS/S	M/L	XL/2XL	3XL/4XL	5XL/6XL
A) Body circumference	in	56.25	64.25	72.25	80.75	88
	cm	143	163.25	183.5	205	223.5
B) Garment length	in	24	24.5	25	25.5	26
	cm	61	62.25	63.5	64.75	66

This poncho is designed with 22–28 inches (56–71 cm) of positive ease. Sample shown is knit in size XS/S.

SCHEMATIC

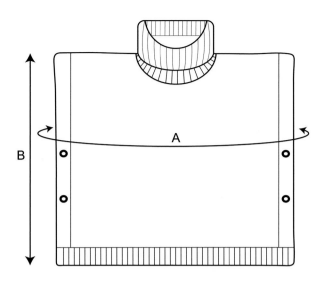

MULBERRY PONCHO PATTERN

FRONT

Using US 8 (5 mm) needles, cast on 168 (188, 208, 232, 252) sts using the longtail cast on method.

Row 1 (WS): Sl1wyib, p1, (k1, p1) 3 times, pm, (k2, p2) until last 8 sts, pm, (k1, p1) 4 times.
Row 2 (RS): Sl1wyib, p1, (k1, p1) 3 times, sm, (k2, p2) until stm, sm, (k1, p1) 4 times.
Repeat the last row until the piece measures 1.75 inches (4.5 cm) from the cast on edge.

Next row (WS): Sl1wyib, p1, (k1, p1) 3 times, sm, p until stm, sm, (k1, p1) 4 times.

MAIN PATTERN

Switch to US 9 (5.5 mm) needles.

Set-up row 1 (RS): Sl1wyib, p1, (k1, p1) 3 times, sm, row 1 of Chart A (page 98–99), pm, k68 (88, 108, 116, 136), pm, row 1 of Chart A, sm, (k1, p1) 4 times.

Set-up row 2 (WS): Sl1wyib, p1, (k1, p1) 3 times, sm, row 2 of Chart A, sm, p until stm, sm, row 2 of Chart A, sm, (k1, p1) 4 times.

Continue working in patt as established until the piece measures 7 inches (17.75 cm) from the cast on edge. Your last row should be a WS row.

Make First Buttonhole (RS): Sl1wyib, p1, k1, p1, yo, k2tog, k1, p1, sm, work in patt until stm, sm, k until stm, sm, work in patt until last stm, sm, k1, p1, k1, yo, k2tog, p1, k1, p1.

> **NOTE:** The yarnover is what creates the buttonhole and should be just the right size for a 1-inch (2.5-cm) button. If you wish to use a larger button, you can experiment and work double yarnovers to create a larger hole. In the following row, you will be treating this yarnover as a regular stitch and knitting into this stitch as usual.

Continue working in patt as established until the piece measures 14 inches (35.5 cm) from the cast on edge. Your last row should be a WS row.

FRONT RIGHT
Row 1 (WS): Work in patt.
Row 2 (RS): K1, ssk, work in patt until end [78 (88, 98, 109, 119) sts rem].
Repeat the last 2 rows 14 more times until 64 (74, 84, 95, 105) sts rem.

Work even until the piece measures 24 (24.5, 25, 25.5, 26) inches / 61 (62.25, 63.5, 64.75, 66) cm from the cast on edge. Your last row should be a RS row. Move rem 64 (74, 84, 95, 105) sts to a holder or spare yarn to return to later. Break the yarn.

FRONT LEFT
Rejoin the yarn to WS of work.

Row 1 (WS): Work in patt.
Row 2 (RS): Work in patt until last 3 sts, k2tog, k1 [78 (88, 98, 109, 119) sts rem].
Repeat the last 2 rows 14 more times until 64 (74, 84, 95, 105) sts rem.

Work even until the piece measures 24 (24.5, 25, 25.5, 26) inches / 61 (62.25, 63.5, 64.75, 66) cm from the cast on edge. Your last row should be a RS row. Ensure your last row matches the last row completed from the front right. Move rem 64 (74, 84, 95, 105) sts to a holder or spare yarn to return to later. Break the yarn.

BACK
Using US 8 (5 mm) needles, cast on 168 (188, 208, 232, 252) sts using the longtail cast on method.

Row 1 (WS): Sl1wyib, p1, (k1, p1) 3 times, pm, (k2, p2) until last 8 sts, pm, (k1, p1) 4 times.
Row 2 (RS): Sl1wyib, p1, (k1, p1) 3 times, sm, (k2, p2) until stm, sm, (k1, p1) 4 times.
Repeat the last row until the piece measures 1.75 inches (4.5 cm) from the cast on edge.

Next row (WS): Sl1wyib, p1, (k1, p1) 3 times, sm, p until stm, sm, (k1, p1) 4 times.

Make Second Buttonhole (RS): Sl1wyib, p1, k1, p1, yo, k2tog, k1, p1, sm, work in patt until stm, sm, k until stm, sm, work in patt until last stm, sm, k1, p1, k1, yo, k2tog, p1, k1, p1.

Work even until the piece measures 18.5 (19, 19.5, 20, 20.5) inches / 47 (48.25, 49.5, 50.75, 52) cm from the cast on edge. Your last row should be a WS row.

Next row (RS): Work 79 (89, 99, 110, 120) sts in patt, bind off 10 (10, 10, 12, 12) sts, work rem 79 (89, 99, 110, 120) sts in patt. Set aside front left sts on a holder or spare yarn to return to later.

TIP: Mark where you left off in the chart.

MAIN PATTERN
Switch to US 9 (5.5 mm) needles.

Set-up row 1 (RS): Sl1wyib, p1, (k1, p1) 3 times, sm, row 1 of Chart A, pm, k68 (88, 108, 116, 136), pm, row 1 of Chart A, sm, (k1, p1) 4 times.
Set-up row 2 (WS): Sl1wyib, p1, (k1, p1) 3 times, sm, row 2 of Chart A, sm, p until stm, sm, row 2 of Chart A, sm, (k1, p1) 4 times.

Continue working in patt as established until you reach 5 rows below where you left off in the front piece. Your last row should be a WS row. The piece should measure approximately 23 (23.5, 24, 24.5, 25) inches / 58.5 (59.75, 61, 62.25, 63.5) cm from the cast on edge.

Next row (RS): Work 66 (76, 86, 97, 107) sts in patt, bind off 36 (36, 36, 38, 38) sts, work rem 66 (76, 86, 97, 107) sts in patt. Set aside back right sts on a holder or spare yarn to return to later.

TIP: Mark where you left off in the chart.

BACK LEFT
Row 1 (WS): Work in patt.
Row 2 (RS): K1, ssk, work in patt until end [65 (75, 85, 96, 106) sts rem].
Row 3: Work in patt.
Row 4: K1, ssk, work in patt until end [64 (74, 84, 95, 105) sts rem].

Place the corresponding front left piece behind the back left piece with the RSs facing each other. Use the 3-needle bind off method to seam the left shoulder. Break the yarn and weave in any loose ends.

BACK RIGHT
Rejoin the yarn to WS of work.

Row 1 (WS): Work in patt.
Row 2 (RS): Work in patt until last 3 sts, k2tog, k1 [65 (75, 85, 96, 106) sts rem].
Row 3: Work in patt.
Row 4: Work in patt until last 3 sts, k2tog, k1 [64 (74, 84, 95, 105) sts rem].

Place the corresponding front right piece behind the back right piece with the RSs facing each other. Use the 3-needle bind off method to seam the right shoulder. Break the yarn and weave in any loose ends.

TURTLENECK
Flip work so the RSs are facing out. Beginning with the left shoulder seam and using US 8 (5 mm) needles, pick up and k29 (approximately 3 sts for every 4 rows) down towards the front, pick up and k10 (10, 10, 12, 12) from the bind off edge, pick up and k29 up towards the right shoulder, pick up and k4 towards the back, pick up and k36 (36, 36, 38, 38) from the bind off edge, and pick up and k4 towards the left shoulder. Pm and join for working in the round [112 (112, 112, 116, 116) sts].

Work in 2x2 ribbing until turtleneck measures 8 inches (20.25 cm) from the pick up edge. Bind off in rib. Weave in any loose ends.

FINISHING
Use removable stms to mark the positions on the back panel edges that correspond to the buttonholes on the front panel. Using the sewing needle and matching thread, attach the buttons to the back panel on both sides.

Weave in any loose ends. Block your project using your preferred method.

MULBERRY PONCHO CABLE CHARTS AND LEGENDS

Chart A Sizes XS–2XL

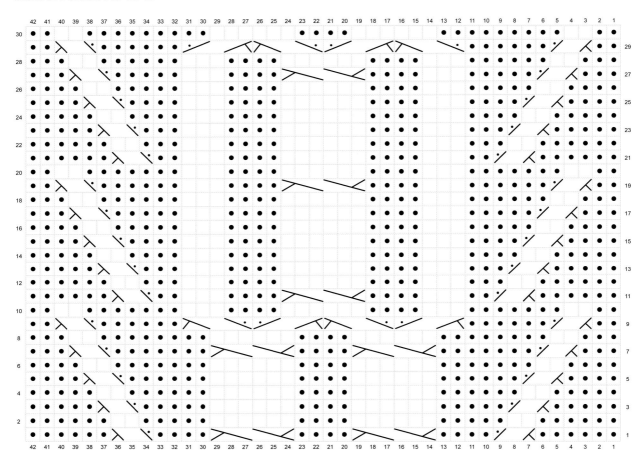

Legend A Sizes XS–2XL

☐		RS: K WS: P
●		RS: P WS: K
╱ ╲		2/1 RPC: slip 1 st to cn and hold in back, k2, p1 from cn
⋏ ⋋		2/1 LPC: slip 2 sts to cn and hold in front, p1, k2 from cn

╱ ╲	3/2 RPC: slip 2 sts to cn and hold in back, k3, p2 from cn
⋏ ╲	3/2 LPC: slip 3 sts to cn and hold in front, p2, k3 from cn
⟋ ⟍	3/3 LC: slip 3 sts to cn and hold in front, k3, k3 from cn

Chart A Sizes 3XL–6XL

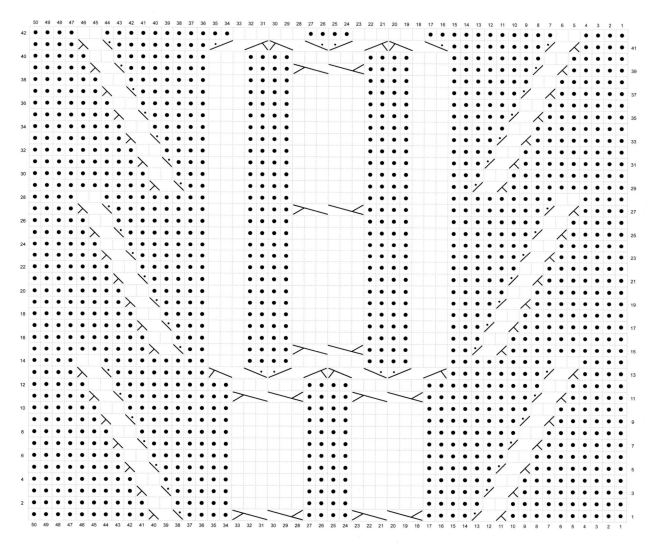

Legend A Sizes 3XL–6XL

		RS: K WS: P
	•	RS: P WS: K
	∕ ∠	2/1 RPC: slip 1 st to cn and hold in back, k2, p1 from cn
	⋋ ⋌	2/1 LPC: slip 2 sts to cn and hold in front, p1, k2 from cn

	⋅∕ ∠	3/2 RPC: slip 2 sts to cn and hold in back, k3, p2 from cn
	⋋ ⋌⋅	3/2 LPC: slip 3 sts to cn and hold in front, p2, k3 from cn
	⋋ ⋌	3/3 LC: slip 3 sts to cn and hold in front, k3, k3 from cn

Willow Pullover

Symbolizing hope and a sense of belonging, the willow tree brings comfort with its delicate but commanding presence. Likewise, the Willow Pullover features simple winding cables inspired by the wavy silhouette of the iconic tree. Designed with bulky weight blown yarn, this billowy sweater will knit up quickly and fly off the needles in no time. The I-cord finishing around the neckline and puff sleeves create an immaculate and professional finish. A boxy, oversized fit ensures maximum comfort with a subdued elegance. Hop on the sweater-over-dress trend by pairing the Willow Pullover with a satin slip skirt and tennis shoes for a casual but feminine look. Accentuate your waist with a statement belt, or simply use the French tuck method to style the sweater with high-waisted pants.

Construction Notes

The pullover begins with an I-cord cast on and is worked from the bottom up in the round before separating for the front and back pieces. The shoulders are joined using the 3-needle bind off method, and stitches are picked up for the neckband and finished with an I-cord edge. Sleeves are picked up and worked in the round from the top down to the cuffs.

SKILL LEVEL
Intermediate

SIZING
XS (S, M, L, XL) (2XL, 3XL, 4XL, 5XL, 6XL)
38.5 (42.5, 46, 50, 53.5) (57.5, 61.25, 65, 68.75, 72.5)" / 97.75 (108, 116.75, 127, 136) (146, 155.5, 165, 174.75, 184.25) cm, blocked

MATERIALS
Yarn
Bulky weight, Wool and the Gang Feeling Good in Ivory White (70% Alpaca, 23% Nylon/Polyamide, 7% Wool), 142 yds (130 m) per 50-g skein

Any bulky weight yarn can be used for this pattern as long as it matches gauge.

Yardage/Meterage
820 (870, 965, 1065, 1280) (1365, 1465, 1555, 1610, 1690) yds / 750 (795, 885, 975, 1170) (1250, 1340, 1425, 1475, 1550) m of bulky weight yarn

Needles
For body: US 10.5 (6.5 mm), 24- to 60-inch (60- to 150-cm) circular needles
For sleeves: US 10.5 (6.5 mm), 16-inch (40-cm) circular or double pointed needles
For neckline and armhole edge: US 8 (5 mm) double pointed needles

Notions
Cable needle
Scissors
Stitch markers
Tapestry needle

GAUGE
18 sts x 20 rounds = 4 inches (10 cm) in reverse stockinette in the round using larger needles (blocked)

TECHNIQUES
3-Needle Bind Off (page 159)
Applied I-cord Edge (explained within the pattern)
I-cord Cast On (page 156)
Longtail Cast On (page 157)

ABBREVIATIONS

0 or -	no stitch / step does not apply to your size
BOR	beginning of round
cn	cable needle
k	knit
k2tog	knit 2 sts together [1 st decreased]
p	purl
p2tog	purl 2 sts together [1 st decreased]
patt	pattern
pm	place marker
rem	remain(ing)
RS	right side
ssk	slip 2 sts knitwise, one at a time; move both stitches back to the left needle; knit these 2 sts together through the back loops [1 st decreased]
ssp	slip 2 sts knitwise, one at a time; move both stitches back to the left needle; purl these 2 sts together through the back loops [1 st decreased]
st(s)	stitch(es)
stm	stitch marker
work(ing) even	continue working the pattern as established without any increases or decreases
WS	wrong side

Cable stitch abbreviations can be found in the Legends on pages 107–108.

SIZING CHART

		XS	S	M	L	XL	2XL	3XL	4XL	5XL	6XL
A) Body circumference	in	38.5	42.5	46	50	53.5	57.5	61.25	65	68.75	72.5
	cm	97.75	108	116.75	127	136	146	155.5	165	174.75	184.25
B) Garment length	in	19	20	20	21	22	23	24	24	26	26
	cm	48.25	50.75	50.75	53.25	56	58.5	61	61	66	66
C) Sleeve circumference	in	14.25	14.25	16	17.75	17.75	19.5	19.5	21.25	21.25	23
	cm	36.25	36.25	40.75	45	45	49.5	49.5	54	54	58.5
D) Sleeve length	in	17	17	17	18	18	18	19	19	20	20
	cm	43.25	43.25	43.25	45.75	45.75	45.75	48.25	48.25	50.75	50.75

This pullover is designed with 6–11 inches (15.25–28 cm) of positive ease. Sample shown is knit in size S.

SCHEMATIC

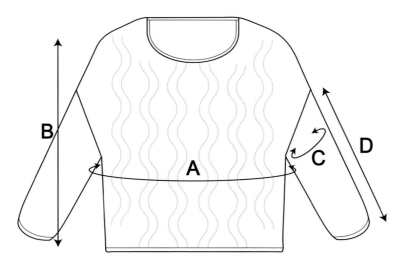

WILLOW PULLOVER PATTERN

BODY

Using US 10.5 (6.5 mm) needles, cast on 164 (180, 196, 212, 228) (244, 260, 276, 292, 308) sts with the I-cord cast on method. Pm and join for working in the round. You may seam the ends of the I-cord now or once the sweater is completed.

K one round.

Sizes XS, S, L, 2XL, 4XL and 6XL only

Set-up round 1: *P1 (5, -, 5, -) (5, -, 5, -, 5), work round 1 of Chart A (page 107), p1 (5, -, 5, -) (5, -, 5, -, 5); repeat from * once more.
Set-up round 2: *P1 (5, -, 5, -) (5, -, 5, -, 5), work round 2 of Chart A, p1 (5, -, 5, -) (5, -, 5, -, 5); repeat from * once more.

Sizes M, XL, 3XL and 5XL only

Set-up round 1: *P1, work round 1 of Chart A (page 108) - (-, 6, -, 7) (-, 8, -, 9, -) times, p1; repeat from * once more.
Set-up round 2: *P1, work round 2 of Chart A - (-, 6, -, 7) (-, 8, -, 9, -) times, p1; repeat from * once more.

All Sizes Resume

Continue working in patt as established until the piece measures 10 (10.5, 10.5, 11, 11) (11.5, 12, 12, 13, 13) inches / 25.5 (26.75, 26.75, 28, 28) (29.25, 30.5, 30.5, 33, 33) cm from the cast on edge. Your last row should be an even numbered row.

Separate for Front/Back

Next row (RS): Work in patt for 82 (90, 98, 106, 114) (122, 130, 138, 146, 154) sts. Turn. Leave rem back sts on a holder or spare yarn to return to later.

TIP: Mark where you left off in the chart.

FRONT

Continue working in patt as established, working back and forth in rows, until the front piece measures 13.5 (14.5, 15, 16, 16.5) (17.5, 18.5, 19, 20.5, 21) inches / 34.25 (36.75, 38, 40.75, 42) (44.5, 47, 48.25, 52, 53.25) cm from the cast on edge. Your last row should be a WS row.

Next row (RS): Work 34 (38, 42, 45, 49) (53, 56, 60, 64, 68) sts in patt, bind off 14 (14, 14, 16, 16) (16, 18, 18, 18, 18) sts, work rem 34 (38, 42, 45, 49) (53, 56, 60, 64, 68) sts in patt. Leave the front left sts on a holder or spare yarn to return to later.

TIP: Mark where you left off in the chart.

FRONT RIGHT

Row 1 (WS): Work in patt.
Row 2 (RS): Bind off 1 st, work in patt until end.
Repeat the last 2 rows 5 more times until 28 (32, 36, 39, 43) (47, 50, 54, 58, 62) sts rem.

NOTE: For cables that no longer have the full amount of sts, you can k those sts on the RS and p on the WS. In instances where only one side of a cable is reduced, continue cabling the remaining side.

Work even until the piece measures 17.5 (18.5, 19, 20, 20.5) (21.5, 22.5, 23, 24.5, 25) inches / 44.5 (47, 48.25, 50.75, 52) (54.5, 57.25, 58.5, 62.25, 63.5) cm from the cast on edge. Your last row should be a WS row. Break the yarn and move live sts to a holder or spare yarn to return to later.

FRONT LEFT

Rejoin the yarn to WS of work.

Row 1 (WS): Bind off 1 st, work in patt until end.
Row 2 (RS): Work in patt.
Repeat the last 2 rows 5 more times until 28 (32, 36, 39, 43) (47, 50, 54, 58, 62) sts rem.

Work even until the piece measures 17.5 (18.5, 19, 20, 20.5) (21.5, 22.5, 23, 24.5, 25) inches / 44.5 (47, 48.25, 50.75, 52) (54.5, 57.25, 58.5, 62.25, 63.5) cm from the cast on edge. Your last row should be a WS row. Break the yarn and move live sts to a holder or spare yarn to return to later.

BACK

Rejoin the yarn to RS of work.

Work even until the piece measures 16.5 (17.5, 18, 19, 19.5) (20.5, 21.5, 22, 23.5, 24) inches / 42 (44.5, 45.75, 48.25, 49.5) (52, 54.5, 56, 59.75, 61) cm from the cast on edge. Your last row should be a WS row.

Next row (RS): Work 30 (34, 38, 41, 45) (49, 52, 56, 60, 64) sts in patt, bind off 22 (22, 22, 24, 24) (24, 26, 26, 26, 26) sts, work rem 30 (34, 38, 41, 45) (49, 52, 56, 60, 64) sts in patt. Leave back right sts on a holder or spare yarn to return to later.

TIP: Mark where you left off in the chart.

BACK LEFT
Row 1 (WS): Work in patt.
Row 2 (RS): Bind off 1 st, work in patt until end.
Repeat the last 2 rows 1 more time until 28 (32, 36, 39, 43) (47, 50, 54, 58, 62) sts rem. Work one more WS row. Do not break the yarn.

Move the front left sts to another needle. Arrange the back and front left pieces so the RSs are facing each other. Use the 3-needle bind off method to seam the shoulders with the back left working yarn. Break the yarn and leave a short tail for weaving in ends.

BACK RIGHT
Rejoin the yarn to WS of work.

Row 1 (WS): Bind off 1 st, work in patt until end.
Row 2 (RS): Work in patt.
Repeat the last 2 rows 1 more time until 28 (32, 36, 39, 43) (47, 50, 54, 58, 62) sts rem. Work one more WS row. Do not break the yarn.

Move the front right sts to another needle. Arrange the back and front right pieces so the RSs are facing each other. Use the 3-needle bind off method to seam the shoulders with the back right working yarn. Break the yarn and leave a short tail for weaving in ends.

Applied I-cord Neckband
Flip work so the RSs are facing out. Using US 8 (5 mm) double pointed needles, cast on 3 sts using the longtail method. Do not turn. Slide the stitches down the double pointed needle to the right end. Bring the working yarn across the back of the sts and k3. Pick up and bind off the neckline sts as described below using the following applied I-cord edge technique:

1. Pick up and knit the next stitch in the neckline [4 sts].
2. Slide the sts to the other end of the needle.
3. Bring the working yarn across the back of the sts. K2, ssk [3 sts rem].

Beginning with the left shoulder, evenly pick up and bind off 20 sts down the left front, 14 (14, 14, 16, 16) (16, 18, 18, 18, 18) sts across the front, 20 sts up towards the right shoulder, and 22 (22, 22, 24, 24) (24, 26, 26, 26, 26) sts across the back.

Break the yarn and seam the ends of the I-cord together.

SLEEVES (MAKE 2)
Using US 10.5 (6.5 mm) needles and beginning with the center of the underarm, evenly pick up and k32 (34, 36, 38, 40) (42, 44, 46, 48, 50) sts towards the shoulder, then evenly pick up and k32 (34, 36, 38, 40) (42, 44, 46, 48, 50) sts towards the underarm. Pm and join for working in the round [64 (68, 72, 76, 80) (84, 88, 92, 96, 100) sts].

Set-up round 1: P0 (2, 4, 6, 0) (2, 4, 6, 0, 2), pm, work round 1 of Chart B (page 108) 4 (4, 4, 4, 5) (5, 5, 5, 6, 6) times, pm, p0 (2, 4, 6, 0) (2, 4, 6, 0, 2).
Set-up round 2: P0 (2, 4, 6, 0) (2, 4, 6, 0, 2), sm, work round 2 of Chart B 4 (4, 4, 4, 5) (5, 5, 5, 6, 6) times, sm, p0 (2, 4, 6, 0) (2, 4, 6, 0, 2).

Continue working in patt as established until the sleeve measures approximately 6 inches (15.25 cm) from the pick up edge.

Begin Decreases

Decrease round: P1, p2tog, continue in patt until last 3 sts, ssp, p1 [62 (66, 70, 74, 78) (82, 86, 90, 94, 98) sts rem, 2 sts decreased].

Work 6 rounds even.

Repeat dec round [60 (64, 68, 72, 76) (80, 84, 88, 92, 96) sts rem].

Sizes 2XL–6XL only
Work 6 rounds even.

Repeat dec round one more time [- (-, -, -, -) (78, 82, 86, 90, 94) sts rem].

All Sizes Resume
Work even until the sleeve measures 17 (17, 17, 18, 18) (18, 19, 19, 20, 20) inches / 43.25 (43.25, 43.25, 45.75, 45.75) (45.75, 48.25, 48.25, 50.75, 50.75) cm from the pick up edge, or until it reaches desired length. Your last round should be an even numbered round.

Decrease round: *K2tog; repeat from * until end [30 (32, 34, 36, 38) (39, 41, 43, 45, 47) sts rem]. Remove BOR stm.

I-cord Sleeve Bind Off
Using a US 8 (5 mm) DPN as your right-hand needle, insert it between the first and second stitch of your left-hand needle. Wrap the working yarn around your needle and draw it up so you have a new stitch. Place the new stitch onto the left-hand needle. Repeat one more time so you have a total of two new stitches.

Next step: K1, ssk from the left needle. Move the 2 sts back to the left needle.

Repeat the last step until no sleeve sts rem. Bind off and seam the ends of the I-cord together.

FINISHING
If you have not already, use the tail yarn from the cast on edge to seam the ends of the I-cord together. Weave in any loose ends. Block your project using your preferred method.

WILLOW PULLOVER CABLE CHARTS AND LEGENDS

Chart A Sizes XS, S, L, 2XL, 4XL, 6XL

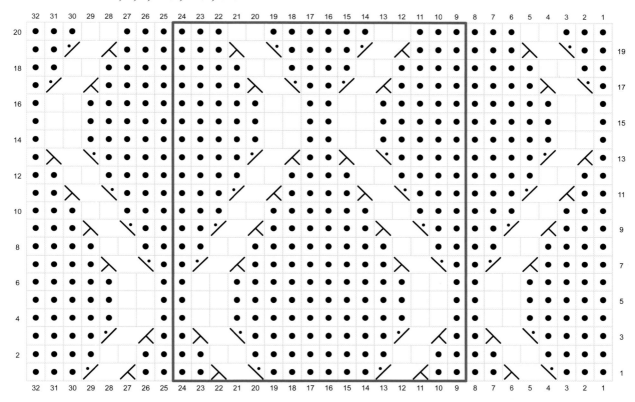

Legend A Sizes XS, S, L, 2XL, 4XL, 6XL

☐	RS: K WS: P
•	RS: P WS: K
⟋ ⟍	2/1 RPC: slip 1 st to cn and hold in back, k2, p1 from cn
⟍ ⟋	2/1 LPC: slip 2 sts to cn and hold in front, p1, k2 from cn
☐	Repeat section 3 (3, -, 4, -) (5, -, 6, -, 7) more times

Chart A Sizes M, XL, 3XL, 5XL

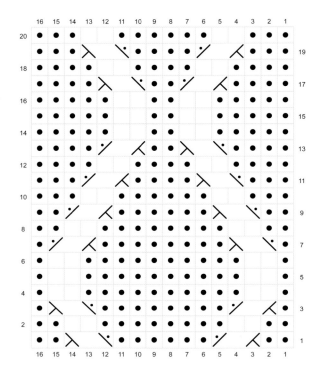

Chart B

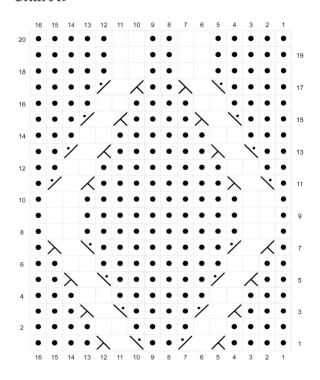

Legend A Sizes M, XL, 3XL, 5XL

☐	RS: K WS: P
●	RS: P WS: K
╱ ╲	2/1 RPC: slip 1 st to cn and hold in back, k2, p1 from cn
⋋ ⋌	2/1 LPC: slip 2 sts to cn and hold in front, p1, k2 from cn

Legend B

☐	k
●	p
╱ ╲	2/1 RPC: slip 1 st to cn and hold in back, k2, p1 from cn
⋋ ⋌	2/1 LPC: slip 2 sts to cn and hold in front, p1, k2 from cn

Sagebrush Sweater

Every wardrobe needs a sweater that is stylish without sacrificing comfort. If I'm being honest, that is practically a requirement in my closet. The Sagebrush Sweater combines the classic stockinette stitch with simple cables to create a generously oversized garment that is equal parts cozy and chic. The cabled yoke provides elegance and visual interest in an otherwise simple crewneck pullover-style garment. To make this sweater, you'll combine a sturdy merino with a mohair halo, creating a fabric that leaves you feeling cozy with a hint of glamor. When warmer weather is on the horizon, slip it over a dress and booties for a charming transitional outfit. You can also opt for a smart casual look by pairing it with a blazer, slim fit pants and tapered flats.

Construction Notes

The sweater is worked from the bottom up in the round. The front and back pieces are then separated and worked flat. The shoulders are seamed using the 3-needle bind off and stitches are picked up for the neckband. Lastly, stitches are picked up around the armholes and the sleeves are worked from the top down in the round.

SKILL LEVEL
Intermediate

SIZING
XS (S, M, L, XL) (2XL, 3XL, 4XL, 5XL, 6XL)
40.5 (44, 50.25, 52, 56.5) (61.75, 64.5, 67, 72.5, 76)" / 102.75 (111.75, 127.75, 132, 143.5) (156.75, 163.75, 170.25, 184.25, 193) cm, blocked

MATERIALS
Yarn
Worsted weight, Knitting for Olive Heavy Merino in Dusty Artichoke (100% Merino Wool), 137 yds (125 m) per 50-g skein *held with*
Lace weight, Knitting for Olive Soft Silk Mohair in Dusty Artichoke (70% Mohair, 30% Silk), 246 yds (225 m) per 25-g skein

Any worsted and lace weight yarn held together can be used for this pattern as long as it matches gauge. If using a single strand of yarn, any bulky weight yarn can be used as long as it matches gauge.

Yardage/Meterage
1365 (1500, 1530, 1570, 1730) (1920, 2020, 2115, 2315, 2445) yds / 1250 (1375, 1400, 1440, 1585) (1760, 1850, 1940, 2120, 2240) m of worsted weight yarn *held with*
1365 (1500, 1530, 1570, 1730) (1920, 2020, 2115, 2315, 2445) yds / 1250 (1375, 1400, 1440, 1585) (1760, 1850, 1940, 2120, 2240) m of textured lace weight yarn

Needles
For ribbing: US 8 (5 mm), 24- to 60-inch (60- to 150-cm) circular needles
For body: US 9 (5.5 mm), 24- to 60-inch (60- to 150-cm) circular needles
For sleeves: US 9 (5.5 mm), 16-inch (40-cm) circular or double pointed needles
For cuffs: US 8 (5 mm), double pointed needles

Notions
Cable needle
Scissors
Stitch markers
Tapestry needle

GAUGE
18 sts x 24 rounds = 4 inches (10 cm) in stockinette stitch in the round using larger needles (blocked)

17 sts x 22 rows = 4 inches (10 cm) in Chart B worked flat using larger needles (blocked)

TECHNIQUES
3-Needle Bind Off (page 159)
Longtail Cast On (page 157)

ABBREVIATIONS

0 or -	no stitch / step does not apply to your size
1x1 ribbing	*k1, p1; repeat from * repeat until end
BOR	beginning of round
cn	cable needle
DPN(s)	double pointed needle(s)
k	knit
k2tog	knit 2 sts together [1 st decreased]
m1l	make 1 left: use the left needle to pick up the strand between the last worked st and the next unworked st from front to back, knit this st through the back loop [1 st increased]
m1r	make 1 right: use the left needle to pick up the strand between the last worked st and the next unworked st from back to front, knit this st through the front loop [1 st increased]
p	purl
patt	pattern
pm	place marker
rem	remain(ing)
RS	right side
sm	slip marker
ssk	slip 2 sts knitwise, one at a time; move both stitches back to the left needle; knit these 2 sts together through the back loops [1 st decreased]
st(s)	stitch(es)
stm	stitch marker
work(ing) even	continue working the pattern as established without any increases or decreases
WS	wrong side
yo	yarnover

Cable stitch abbreviations can be found in the Legends on pages 116–117.

SCHEMATIC

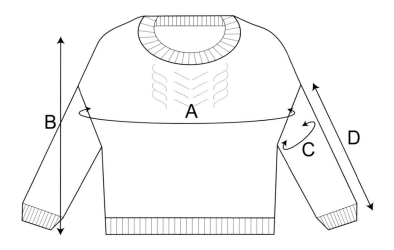

SIZING CHART

		XS	S	M	L	XL	2XL	3XL	4XL	5XL	6XL
A) Body circumference	in	40.5	44	50.25	52	56.5	61.75	64.5	67	72.5	76
	cm	102.75	111.75	127.75	132	143.5	156.75	163.75	170.25	184.25	193
B) Garment length	in	24	24.5	25	25.5	26	26.5	27	27.5	28	28.5
	cm	61	62.25	63.5	64.75	66	67.25	68.5	69.75	71	72.5
C) Sleeve circumference	in	15	16	17	17.75	19	20	21	21.75	23	24
	cm	38	40.75	43.25	45	48.25	50.75	53.25	55.25	58.5	61
D) Sleeve length	in	16.5	17	17.5	19	19	19	19.5	19.5	20	20.5
	cm	42	43.25	44.5	48.25	48.25	48.25	49.5	49.5	50.75	52

This sweater is designed with 9–14 inches (22.75–35.5 cm) of positive ease. Sample shown is knit in size XS.

SAGEBRUSH SWEATER PATTERN

BODY

Using US 8 (5 mm) circular needles, cast on 85 (93, 107, 111, 121) (133, 139, 145, 157, 165) sts using the longtail cast on method, pm for side, cast on another 85 (93, 107, 111, 121) (133, 139, 145, 157, 165) sts using the longtail cast on method. Pm and join for working in the round [170 (186, 214, 222, 242) (266, 278, 290, 314, 330) sts].

Work in 1x1 ribbing for 1.5 inches (3.75 cm).

Switch to US 9 (5.5 mm) needles.

K all rounds until the piece measures 12.5 inches (31.75 cm) from the cast on edge.

Begin Underarm Shaping

Round 1: *K1, m1l, k until 1 st before side marker, m1r, k1, sm; repeat from * once more [174 (190, 218, 226, 246) (270, 282, 294, 318, 334) sts].
Rounds 2–4: K all.
Repeat rounds 1–4 two more times [182 (198, 226, 234, 254) (278, 290, 302, 326, 342) sts].

Separate for Front/Back

Next row (RS): Remove BOR stm. K0 (3, 0, 0, 5) (0, 2, 5, 0, 3), p1 (2, 0, 2, 2) (1, 2, 2, 1, 2), row 1 of Chart A (page 116) 3 (3, 4, 4, 4) (5, 5, 5, 6, 6) times, row 1 of Chart B (page 116), row 1 of Chart C (page 117) 3 (3, 4, 4, 4) (5, 5, 5, 6, 6) times, p1 (2, 0, 2, 2) (1, 2, 2, 1, 2), k0 (3, 0, 0, 5) (0, 2, 5, 0, 3). Turn work and leave rem back sts on a holder or spare yarn to return to later.

FRONT

Next row (WS): P0 (3, 0, 0, 5) (0, 2, 5, 0, 3), k1 (2, 0, 2, 2) (1, 2, 2, 1, 2), row 2 of Chart C 3 (3, 4, 4, 4) (5, 5, 5, 6, 6) times, row 2 of Chart B, row 2 of Chart A 3 (3, 4, 4, 4) (5, 5, 5, 6, 6) times, k1 (2, 0, 2, 2) (1, 2, 2, 1, 2), p0 (3, 0, 0, 5) (0, 2, 5, 0, 3).

Continue working in patt as established until the piece measures 20 (20.5, 21, 21.5, 22) (22.5, 23, 23.5, 24, 24.5) inches / 50.75 (52, 53.25, 54.5, 56) (57.25, 58.5, 59.75, 61, 62.25) cm from the cast on edge. Your last row should be a WS row.

Next row (RS): Work 37 (41, 48, 50, 55) (60, 63, 66, 72, 76) sts in patt, bind off 17 (17, 17, 17, 17) (19, 19, 19, 19, 19) sts, work rem 37 (41, 48, 50, 55) (60, 63, 66, 72, 76) sts in patt. Turn and leave left shoulder sts on a holder or spare yarn to return to later.

TIP: Mark where you left off in the charts.

FRONT LEFT SHOULDER

Rejoin the yarn to WS of work.

Row 1 (WS): Bind off 1 st, work in patt until end [36 (40, 47, 49, 54) (59, 62, 65, 71, 75) sts rem].

Row 2 (RS): Work in patt.

Repeat rows 1 and 2 a total of 9 more times until 27 (31, 38, 40, 45) (50, 53, 56, 62, 66) rem. Break the yarn and move live sts to a holder or spare yarn to return to later.

BACK

Rejoin the yarn to RS of work.

Set-up row 1 (RS): K0 (3, 0, 0, 5) (0, 2, 5, 0, 3), p1 (2, 0, 2, 2) (1, 2, 2, 1, 2), row 1 of Chart A 3 (3, 4, 4, 4) (5, 5, 5, 6, 6) times, row 1 of Chart B, row 1 of Chart C 3 (3, 4, 4, 4) (5, 5, 5, 6, 6) times, p1 (2, 0, 2, 2) (1, 2, 2, 1, 2), k0 (3, 0, 0, 5) (0, 2, 5, 0, 3).

Set-up row 2 (WS): P0 (3, 0, 0, 5) (0, 2, 5, 0, 3), k1 (2, 0, 2, 2) (1, 2, 2, 1, 2), row 2 of Chart C 3 (3, 4, 4, 4) (5, 5, 5, 6, 6) times, row 2 of Chart B, row 2 of Chart A 3 (3, 4, 4, 4) (5, 5, 5, 6, 6) times, k1 (2, 0, 2, 2) (1, 2, 2, 1, 2), p0 (3, 0, 0, 5) (0, 2, 5, 0, 3).

Continue working in patt as established until the piece measures 23 (23.5, 24, 24.5, 25) (25.5, 26, 26.5, 27, 27.5) inches / 58.5 (59.75, 61, 62.25, 63.5) (64.75, 66, 67.25, 68.5, 69.75) cm from the cast on edge. Your last row should be a WS row.

Next row (RS): Work 29 (33, 40, 42, 47) (52, 55, 58, 64, 68) sts in patt, bind off 33 (33, 33, 33, 33) (35, 35, 35, 35, 35) sts, work rem 29 (33, 40, 42, 47) (52, 55, 58, 64, 68) sts in patt.

Turn and leave back right shoulder sts on a holder or spare yarn to return to later.

TIP: Mark where you left off in the charts.

FRONT RIGHT SHOULDER

Row 1 (WS): Work in patt.

Row 2 (RS): Bind off 1 st, work in patt until end [36 (40, 47, 49, 54) (59, 62, 65, 71, 75) sts rem]. Repeat rows 1 and 2 a total of 9 more times until 27 (31, 38, 40, 45) (50, 53, 56, 62, 66) rem. Break the yarn and move live sts to a holder or spare yarn to return to later.

BACK LEFT SHOULDER

Row 1 (WS): Work in patt.
Row 2 (RS): Bind off 1 st, work in patt until end [28 (32, 39, 41, 46) (51, 54, 57, 63, 67) sts rem]. Repeat rows 1 and 2 one more time until 27 (31, 38, 40, 45) (50, 53, 56, 62, 66) rem. Break the yarn, leaving a tail that is three times the length of the shoulder. Move live sts to a holder or spare yarn to return to later.

BACK RIGHT SHOULDER

Rejoin the yarn to WS of work.
Row 1 (WS): Bind off 1 st, work in patt until end [28 (32, 39, 41, 46) (51, 54, 57, 63, 67) sts rem].
Row 2 (RS): Work in patt.
Repeat rows 1 and 2 one more time until 27 (31, 38, 40, 45) (50, 53, 56, 62, 66) rem. Break the yarn, leaving a tail that is three times the length of the shoulder.

Join Shoulders

Move the front right shoulder to another needle to prepare for bind off. Flip your work so the RSs are facing each other and use the 3-needle bind off to join the shoulders. Repeat step for the left shoulder.

NECKBAND

Flip work so the RSs are facing out. Using US 8 (5 mm) circular needles and beginning with the left shoulder seam, evenly pick up and k13 down towards the front, pick up and k17 (17, 17, 17, 17) (19, 19, 19, 19, 19) from the front bind off, evenly pick up and k13 towards the right shoulder, evenly pick up and k3 towards the back, pick up and k33 (33, 33, 33, 33) (35, 35, 35, 35, 35) from the back bind off, and evenly pick up and k3 towards the left shoulder. Pm and join for working in the round [82 (82, 82, 82, 82) (86, 86, 86, 86, 86) sts].

Work in 1x1 ribbing for 6 rounds. Bind off in rib.

SLEEVES (MAKE 2)

Using US 9 (5.5 mm) circular needles or DPNs and beginning with the center of the underarm, evenly pick up and k34 (36, 38, 40, 43) (45, 47, 49, 52, 54) towards the shoulder, then evenly pick up and k34 (36, 38, 40, 43) (45, 47, 49, 52, 54) back towards the underarm. Pm and join for working in the round [68 (72, 76, 80, 86) (90, 94, 98, 104, 108) sts].

K all rounds until the sleeve measures 7 (7, 4.5, 4.5, 4) (4, 4, 4, 3.5, 3.5) inches / 17.75 (17.75, 11.5, 11.5, 10.25) (10.25, 10.25, 10.25, 9, 9) cm from the pick up edge.

Decrease round: K1, k2tog, k until last 3 sts, ssk, k1 [66 (70, 74, 78, 84) (88, 92, 96, 102, 106) sts rem].

Repeat dec round every 8th (8th, 7th, 7th, 6th) (5th, 5th, 5th, 4th, 4th) round 2 (3, 5, 6, 5) (8, 9, 8, 8, 9) more times, then every 7th (7th, 6th, 6th, 5th) (4th, 4th, 4th, 4th, 4th) round 4 (5, 5, 6, 9) (8, 9, 7, 8, 8) more times, then every 0th (0th, 0th, 0th, 0th) (0th, 0th, 3rd, 3rd, 3rd) round 0 (0, 0, 0, 0) (0, 0, 5, 7, 8) more times [54 (54, 54, 54, 56) (56, 56, 56, 56, 56) sts rem].

Work even until the sleeve measures 15 (15.5, 16, 17.5, 17.5) (17.5, 18, 18, 18.5, 19) inches / 38 (39.25, 40.75, 44.5, 44.5) (44.5, 45.75, 45.75, 47, 48.25) cm from the pick up edge, or until it reaches desired length.

Switch to US 8 (5 mm) circular needles or DPNs.

Work in 1x1 rib for 1.5 inches (3.75 cm). Bind off in patt.

FINISHING

Weave in any loose ends. Block your project using your preferred method.

SAGEBRUSH SWEATER CABLE CHARTS AND LEGENDS

Chart A

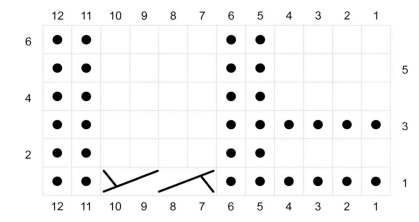

Legend A

		RS: K WS: P
	•	RS: P WS: K
		2/2 RC: slip 2 sts to cn and hold in back, k2, k2 from cn

Chart B

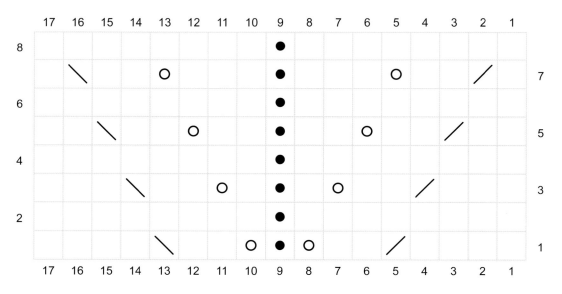

Legend B

☐	RS: K WS: P
•	RS: P WS: K
╱	k2tog
╲	ssk
○	yo

Legend C

☐	RS: K WS: P
•	RS: P WS: K
⟋⟍⟍	2/2 LC: slip 2 sts to cn and hold in front, k2, k2 from cn.

Chart C

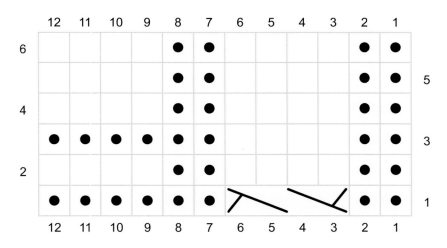

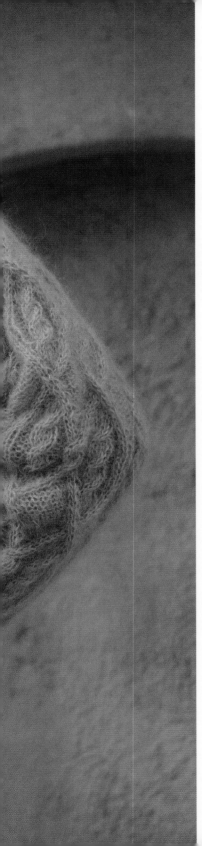

LIGHT & BREATHABLE

Lightweight & Airy Garments

If you think knitwear is just for staying cozy, you're missing out. The growing popularity of knitwear beyond the winter months has been one of the most exciting trends in fashion in recent years. Dispel the notion that knitting is only a cold weather hobby and indulge in the world of cotton, fine merino and mulberry silk. This chapter explores designs knit with lace- to DK-weight yarns, creating lightweight fabrics that feel airy and breathable next to the skin. The result? Cable patterns that, when knit at a finer gauge, appear even more delicate, intricate and visually interesting.

With matching sets becoming ever so popular, the Azalea Top (page 127) and Azalea Cardigan (page 135) were designed to create an effortless ensemble for a day out. Alternatively, break up the pieces for a completely different look. If strapless is your vibe, the Magnolia Top (page 121) is a fun and flirty option that knits up quicker than it looks due to its repetitive pattern. The Rosemary Sweater (page 147), while not your traditional warm-weather garment, makes you feel like you're wearing a cloud. Whether wearing these designs as standalone garments or layered with outerwear, you'll stun without feeling weighed down.

Magnolia Top

Liberate your shoulders with a handknit strapless top that is the perfect blend of sweet and sultry. With a simple, strapless cut that flows across the chest and accentuates the shoulders and collarbones, the Magnolia Top is a feminine and flirty addition to any warm weather wardrobe. Magnolias represent perseverance and longevity, and the repetitive cabling is my way of honoring the stunning blooms of this beloved flower. The top is held up by an elastic that hugs the chest, with a peplum that accentuates the waist and flatters any figure. The body features a cable and lace detailing for added dimension. Lovely as a layer or effortlessly styled solo, this top is designed to take you from a casual day out all the way to the dance floor.

Construction Notes

The top is worked from the top down in the round, beginning with a folded hem. The body is continued in the round until increases are made for the peplum. The peplum is finished with an I-cord bind off. Lastly, an elastic is inserted into the folded hem to provide extra stability and to keep the tube top from falling!

SKILL LEVEL
Intermediate

SIZING
XS (S, M, L, XL) (2XL, 3XL, 4XL, 5XL, 6XL)
29.25 (33.75, 36, 40.5, 45) (49.5, 54, 56.25, 60.75, 65.25)" / 74.25 (85.75, 91.5, 102.75, 114.25) (125.75, 137.25, 143, 154.25, 165.75) cm, blocked

MATERIALS
Yarn
Fingering weight, Knitting for Olive Merino in Dusty Rose (100% Extra Fine Merino), 273 yds (250 m) per 50-g skein

Any fingering weight yarn can be used for this pattern as long as it matches gauge.

Yardage/Meterage
645 (750, 800, 895, 1000) (1105, 1200, 1250, 1355, 1450) yds / 590 (685, 730, 820, 915) (1010, 1100, 1145, 1240, 1330) m of fingering weight yarn

Needles
For folded hem and peplum: US 2 (2.75 mm), 24- to 60-inch (60- to 150-cm) circular needles
For body: US 2.5 (3 mm), 24- to 60-inch (60- to 150-cm) circular needles
For I-cord bind off: US 2 (2.75 mm) double pointed needles

Notions
0.75" (2-cm) elastic (length required is 8" [20.25 cm] less than your upper bust)
Cable needle
Sewing needle and thread
Safety pin
Scissors
Stitch marker(s)
Tapestry needle

GAUGE
32 sts x 40 rounds = 4 inches (10 cm) in stockinette st in the round using smaller needles (blocked)

32 sts x 40 rounds = 4 inches (10 cm) in Chart A in the round using larger needles (blocked)

TECHNIQUES
Backwards Loop Cast On (page 155)
I-cord Bind Off (explained within the pattern)
Longtail Cast On (page 157)
Whip Stitch (page 162)

ABBREVIATIONS

BOR	beginning of round
cn	cable needle
DPN(s)	double pointed needle(s)
k	knit
k2tog	knit 2 sts together [1 st decreased]
k2togtbl	knit 2 sts together through the back loop [1 st decreased]
m1b	make 1 below: insert right needle into the st below the next st, k1; k into the next st normally [1 st increased]
p	purl
patt	pattern
pm	place marker
rem	remain(ing)
RS	right side
st(s)	stitch(es)
WS	wrong side
yo	yarnover

Cable stitch abbreviations can be found in the Legend on page 125.

SIZING CHART

		XS	S	M	L	XL	2XL	3XL	4XL	5XL	6XL
A) Body circumfer-ence	in	29.25	33.75	36	40.5	45	49.5	54	56.25	60.75	65.25
	cm	74.25	85.75	91.5	102.75	114.25	125.75	137.25	143	154.25	165.75
B) Garment length	in	14	14.5	14.5	15	15.5	15.5	16	16.5	16.5	17
	cm	35.5	36.75	36.75	38	39.25	39.25	40.75	42	42	43.25

This top is designed with neutral ease. Sample shown is knit in size XS. If you are in between sizes, select the smaller size.

SCHEMATIC

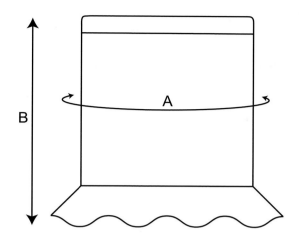

MAGNOLIA TOP PATTERN

BODY

Using US 2 (2.75 mm) needles, cast on 208 (240, 256, 288, 320) (352, 384, 400, 432, 464) sts using the longtail cast on method. Pm and join for working in the round.

Rounds 1–8: K all sts.
Round 9: P all sts.
Rounds 10–18: K all sts.

Create Folded Hem

Fold your work so the purl round is now the bottom. Pick up the corresponding st from the cast on edge and place on left needle. K it together with the st from the current round. Repeat until you reach 4 sts before the BOR marker, k4 from the current round. This will leave a small opening for you to insert an elastic afterwards.

Next round: *M1b, k8; repeat from * until end [234 (270, 288, 324, 360) (396, 432, 450, 486, 522) sts].

MAIN PATTERN

Switch to US 2.5 (3 mm) needles.

Round 1: *P2, k6, p2, k2, p1, yo, k2tog, p1, k2; repeat from * until end.
Round 2: *P2, k6, p2, k2, p1, k2, p1, k2; repeat from * until end.
Round 3: *P2, k6, p2, k2, p1, k2tog, yo, p1, k2; repeat from * until end.
Round 4: *P2, k6, p2, k2, p1, k2, p1, k2; repeat from * until end.
Round 5: *P2, 3/3 RC, p2, k2, p1, yo, k2tog, p1, k2; repeat from * until end.
Round 6: *P2, k6, p2, k2, p1, k2, p1, k2; repeat from * until end.
Round 7: *P2, k6, p2, k2, p1, k2tog, yo, p1, k2; repeat from * until end.
Round 8: *P2, k6, p2, k2, p1, k2, p1, k2; repeat from * until end.

The cable and lace pattern is also provided in chart format (Chart A [page 125]).

Repeat rounds 1–8 until the piece measures 11.5 (12, 12, 12.5, 13) (13, 13.5, 14, 14, 14.5) inches / 29.25 (30.5, 30.5, 31.75, 33) (33, 34.25, 35.5, 35.5, 36.75) cm from the purl round of the folded hem, or until it reaches desired length. Your last round should be an even numbered round. If possible, avoid ending on round 6 of the cable chart to prevent puckering from the cable patt being too close to the edge.

Peplum

K 1 round.

Increase round: *M1b, k1; repeat from * until end [468 (540, 576, 648, 720) (792, 864, 900, 972, 1044) sts].

K all rounds until the peplum measures 2.5 inches (6.5 cm) from the inc round. Remove BOR marker.

I-cord Bind Off

With the RS still facing you, use the backwards loop cast on method to cast on 1 st to your right needle. Turn work. You will be working the I-cord on the WS of the top. You will now be using a US 2 (2.75 mm) DPN as your right-hand needle.

Next row: K1, k2togtbl. You will now have 2 sts on your right-hand needle. Note, the second st in the 'k2togtbl' is a live stitch from the peplum edge. Move these 2 sts back to your left needle. Repeat these two steps until all sts have been worked. When you have two sts remaining, slip the second st over the last st and tie off.

Leave a tail long enough to weave in any ends, so there are no gaps from the beginning and end of the I-cord bind off.

FINISHING

Block your project using your preferred method.

Measure a piece of elastic to your preferred length (at least 8 inches [20.25 cm] less than your upper bust is a good starting point). Keep in mind elastic bands become looser with time.

Use a safety pin to insert and guide the elastic through the folded hem. When the ends of your elastic meet, use your sewing needle and thread to sew the ends together. Use the whip stitch technique to close the final gap and enclose your elastic into the folded hem. Tie off and weave in any loose ends.

MAGNOLIA TOP CABLE CHART A

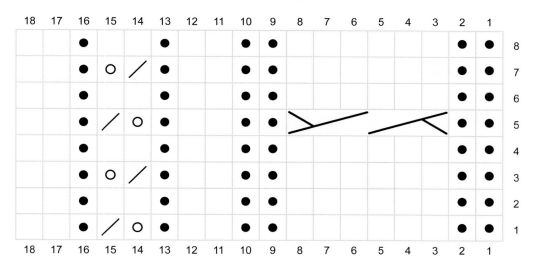

LEGEND

Symbol	Meaning
	k
•	p
o	yo
/	k2tog
⟩—⟨	3/3 RC: slip 3 sts to cn and hold in back, k3, k3 from cn

Azalea Top

Inspired by the athleisure trend, the Azalea Top highlights the shoulder blades and back with a flattering racerback cut. With warm weather in mind, I chose a plant-based fiber blend to complement the dense cables while still keeping the top relatively lightweight.

With delicate cables and textures, the Azalea Top is designed to mirror the unique attributes of its namesake flower. The diamond cables reflect the pointed petals, while the traveling twisted stitches and bobbles mimic the stamen of the flower. The top is stylish yet practical: The neckline is low enough to style the top with a statement necklace, and the cross-back straps can be customized to your preferred length and are thick enough to hide away any bra straps.

Construction Notes

The top is worked in the round from the bottom up before separating for the front and back pieces and working flat. The back is shaped using a series of decreases, and the front is finished with a ribbing. Finally, the double stockinette stitch straps are worked and then joined to the back to form the racerback. **Note:** Sizes L–3XL begin and end with Chart B rather than Chart A.

SKILL LEVEL
Intermediate

SIZING
XS (S, M, L, XL) (2XL, 3XL, 4XL, 5XL, 6XL)
28.25 (32.75, 37.25, 40.25, 44.75) (49, 52,
57.25, 60.25, 64.75)" / 71.75 (83.25, 94.5,
102.25, 113.75) (124.5, 132, 145.5, 153, 164.5)
cm, blocked

MATERIALS
Yarn
DK weight, Stitch & Story Secret Garden in Lily White (60% Cotton, 40% Acrylic), 218 yds (200 m) per 100-g skein

Any DK weight yarn can be used for this pattern as long as it matches gauge.

Yardage/Meterage
390 (440, 500, 540, 600) (645, 750, 765, 830, 840) yds / 355 (400, 455, 495, 550) (590, 685, 700, 760, 770) m of DK weight yarn

Needles
For lower ribbing and body: US 6 (4 mm), 24- to 60-inch (60- to 150-cm) circular needles
For upper ribbing and straps: US 4 (3.5 mm), straight or circular needles

Notions
Cable needle
Scissors
Stitch marker(s)
Tapestry needle

GAUGE
21.5 sts x 32 rounds = 4 inches (10 cm) in moss stitch in the round using larger needle (blocked)

25 sts x 32 rounds = 4 inches (10 cm) in Chart A in the round using larger needle (blocked)

TECHNIQUES
3-Needle Bind Off (page 159)
Longtail Cast On (page 157)
Moss Stitch (page 162)

ABBREVIATIONS

0 or -	no stitch / step does not apply to your size
1x1 ribbing	*k1, p1; repeat from * repeat until end
BOR	beginning of round
cn	cable needle
k	knit
k1tbl	knit through the back loop
k2tog	knit two stitches together [1 st decreased]
kfb	knit front back: knit into the next st without sliding the st off the left-hand needle. Insert tip of the right-hand needle into the back loop of the same st and knit through the back loop. Slide sts off [1 st increased]
p	purl
p1tbl	purl through the back loop
p2tog	purl 2 sts together [1 st decreased]
patt	pattern
pm	place marker
rem	remain(ing)
RS	right side
sl1wyib	slip 1 st purlwise with yarn in back
sl1wyif	slip 1 st purlwise with yarn in front
sl2wyib	slip 2 sts purlwise with yarn in back
st(s)	stitch(es)
stm	stitch marker
work(ing) even	continue working the pattern as established without any increases or decreases
WS	wrong side
yo	yarnover

Cable stitch abbreviations can be found in the Legends on pages 133–134.

SCHEMATIC

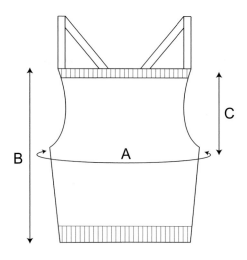

SIZING CHART

		XS	S	M	L	XL	2XL	3XL	4XL	5XL	6XL
A) Body circumference	in	28.25	32.75	37.25	40.25	44.75	49	52	57.25	60.25	64.75
	cm	71.75	83.25	94.5	102.25	113.75	124.5	132	145.5	153	164.5
B) Garment length (from ribbing to front hem)	in	14	14	14.5	14.5	15	15	15.5	16	16	16.5
	cm	35.5	35.5	36.75	36.75	38	38	39.25	40.75	40.75	42
C) Height of front panel after split	in	4.5	5	5	5.5	5.5	5.5	5.5	6	6	6.5
	cm	11.5	12.75	12.75	14	14	14	14	15.25	15.25	16.5

This top is designed with 0–2 inches (0–5 cm) of negative ease to 0–2 inches (0–5 cm) of positive ease.

Two samples are shown: A size S sample shown in Lily White is worn with 2 inches (5 cm) of positive ease, and a size XS sample shown in Light Yellow (We Are Knitters Pima Cotton) is worn with 2 inches (5 cm) of negative ease.

AZALEA TOP PATTERN

BODY

Using US 6 (4 mm) needles, cast on 136 (152, 176, 200, 216) (240, 256, 292, 300, 324) sts using the longtail cast on method. Pm and join for working in the round.

Work in 1x1 ribbing for 1.5 inches (3.75 cm).

K one round.

Sizes XS–M only

Set-up round 1: *(k1, p1) 1 (3, 6, -, -) (-, -, -, -, -) times, work round 1 of Chart A (page 133), work round 1 of Chart B (page 134), work round 1 of Chart A, (k1, p1) 1 (3, 6, -, -) (-, -, -, -, -) times; pm and repeat from * once more.

Set-up round 2: *(k1, p1) 1 (3, 6, -, -) (-, -, -, -, -) times, work round 2 of Chart A, work round 2 of Chart B, work round 2 of Chart A, (k1, p1) 1 (3, 6, -, -) (-, -, -, -, -) times; sm, repeat from * once more.

Set-up round 3: *(p1, k1) 1 (3, 6, -, -) (-, -, -, -, -) times, work round 3 of Chart A, work round 3 of Chart B, work round 3 of Chart A, (p1, k1) 1 (3, 6, -, -) (-, -, -, -, -) times; sm, repeat from * once more.

Set-up round 4: *(p1, k1) 1 (3, 6, -, -) (-, -, -, -, -) times, work round 4 of Chart A, work round 4 of Chart B, work round 4 of Chart A, (p1, k1) 1 (3, 6, -, -) (-, -, -, -, -) times; sm, repeat from * once more.

Sizes L–3XL only

Set-up round 1: *(k1, p1) - (-, -, 1, 3) (6, 8, -, -, -) times, p2, work round 1 of Chart B (page 134), work round 1 of Chart A (page 133), work round 1 of Chart B, work round 1 of Chart A, work round 1 of Chart B, p2, (k1, p1) - (-, -, 1, 3) (6, 8, -, -, -) times; pm and repeat from * once more.

Set-up round 2: *(k1, p1) - (-, -, 1, 3) (6, 8, -, -, -) times, p2, work round 2 of Chart B, work round 2 of Chart A, work round 2 of Chart B, work round 2 of Chart A, work round 2 of Chart B, p2, (k1, p1) - (-, -, 1, 3) (6, 8, -, -, -) times; sm, repeat from * once more.

Set-up round 3: *(p1, k1) - (-, -, 1, 3) (6, 8, -, -, -) times, p2, work round 3 of Chart B, work round 3 of Chart A, work round 3 of Chart B, work round 3 of Chart A, work round 3 of Chart B, p2, (p1, k1) - (-, -, 1, 3) (6, 8, -, -, -) times; sm, repeat from * once more.

Set-up round 4: *(p1, k1) - (-, -, 1, 3) (6, 8, -, -, -) times, p2, work round 4 of Chart B, work round 4 of Chart A, work round 4 of Chart B, work round 4 of Chart A, work round 4 of Chart B, p2, (p1, k1) - (-, -, 1, 3) (6, 8, -, -, -) times; sm, repeat from * once more.

Sizes 4XL–6XL only

Set-up round 1: *(k1, p1) - (-, -, -, -) (-, -, 1, 2, 5) times, work round 1 of Chart A (page 133), work round 1 of Chart B (page 134), work round 1 of Chart A, work round 1 of Chart B, work round 1 of Chart A, (k1, p1) - (-, -, -, -) (-, -, 1, 2, 5) times; pm and repeat from * once more.

Set-up round 2: *(k1, p1) - (-, -, -, -) (-, -, 1, 2, 5) times, work round 2 of Chart A, work round 2 of Chart B, work round 2 of Chart A, work round 2 of Chart B, work round 2 of Chart A, (k1, p1) - (-, -, -, -) (-, -, 1, 2, 5) times; sm, repeat from * once more.

Set-up round 3: *(p1, k1) - (-, -, -, -) (-, -, 1, 2, 5) times, work round 3 of Chart A, work round 3 of Chart B, work round 3 of Chart A, work round 3 of Chart B, work round 3 of Chart A, (p1, k1) - (-, -, -, -) (-, -, 1, 2, 5) times; sm, repeat from * once more.

Set-up round 4: *(p1, k1) - (-, -, -, -) (-, -, 1, 2, 5) times, work round 4 of Chart A, work round 4 of Chart B, work round 4 of Chart A, work round 4 of Chart B, work round 4 of Chart A, (p1, k1) - (-, -, -, -) (-, -, 1, 2, 5) times; sm, repeat from * once more.

All Sizes Resume

Work even until the piece measures 4 inches (10 cm) from the cast on edge. Your last round should be round 4 of the moss st patt. The following increases take place across multiple rounds. The moss stitch pattern will be properly aligned after the second round of increases in round 5.

Round 1 (increase): *Kfb, work in patt until 1 st before the side marker, kfb; repeat from * once more [140 (156, 180, 204, 220) (244, 260, 296, 304, 328) sts].
Rounds 2–4: Work in patt.
Round 5 (increase): *Kfb, work in patt until 1 st before the side marker, kfb; repeat from * once more [144 (160, 184, 208, 224) (248, 264, 300, 308, 332) sts].
Rounds 6–8: Work in patt.
Repeat rounds 1–8 a total of 1 (2, 2, 1, 2) (2, 2, 1, 2, 2) more times [152 (176, 200, 216, 240) (264, 280, 308, 324, 348) sts].

Work even until the piece measures 9.5 (9.5, 10, 10.5, 11) (11.5, 12, 12, 13, 14) inches / 24.25 (24.25, 25.5, 26.75, 28) (29.25, 30.5, 30.5, 33, 35.5) cm from the cast on edge. Your last round should be an even numbered round.

NOTE: Missed a bobble? Not to worry, you can knit one separately and sew it on afterwards. All you have to do is make a slipknot and follow the rest of the instructions for making a bobble. Break the yarn, leaving approximately a 3-inch (7.5-cm) tail. Close the stitch by threading the tail through it. Fasten the bobble into place.

Separate for Front/Back

Next row (RS): Remove BOR stm, bind off 3 (4, 4, 4, 6) (6, 6, 6, 8, 8) sts, work in patt until side stm. Remove side stm and turn. Leave rem back sts on a holder or spare yarn to return to later [73 (84, 96, 104, 114) (126, 134, 148, 154, 166) sts rem].

TIP: Mark where you left off in the charts.

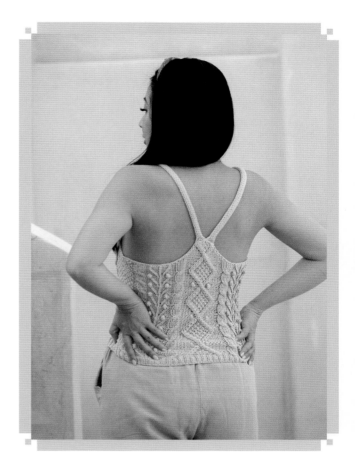

Next row (WS): Bind off 3 (4, 4, 4, 6) (6, 6, 6, 8, 8) sts, work in patt until last st, sl1wyif [70 (80, 92, 100, 108) (120, 128, 142, 146, 158) sts rem].

FRONT

Row 1 (RS): Sl2wyib, slip first st over the next st as if to bind off. Tighten gently and work in patt until last st, sl1wyif [69 (79, 91, 99, 107) (119, 127, 141, 145, 157) sts rem].
Row 2 (WS): Sl2wyib, slip first st over the next st as if to bind off. Tighten gently and work in patt until last st, sl1wyif [68 (78, 90, 98, 106) (118, 126, 140, 144, 156) sts rem].
Repeat rows 1 and 2 a total of 1 (5, 5, 3, 5) (5, 5, 5, 1, 5) more times [66 (68, 80, 92, 96) (108, 116, 130, 142, 146) sts rem].

Next row (RS): Sl1wyif, work in patt until last st, k1.
Next row (WS): Sl1wyif, work in patt until last st, k1.

Work even, slipping the first st of every row, until the piece measures 13 (13.5, 14, 15, 15.5) (16, 16.5, 17, 18, 19.5) inches / 33 (34.25, 35.5, 38, 39.25) (40.75, 42, 43.25, 45.75, 49.5) cm from the cast on edge. Your last row should be a WS row.

Front Hem Ribbing
Switch to US 4 (3.5 mm) needles. Beginning on the RS, work in 1x1 ribbing for 1 inch (2.5 cm). Your last row should be a WS row.

Next row (RS): (K1, sl1wyif) 3 times. Place the 6 sts you just worked onto a holder or spare yarn to return to later. Tightly bind off all rem sts until 6 sts rem, (k1, sl1wyif) 3 times. Turn.

RIGHT STRAP
Switch to US 4 (3.5 mm) needles.

Next row (WS): (K1, sl1wyif) 3 times. Turn. Repeat the last row until strap measures approximately 12 inches (30.5 cm), or desired length. Break the yarn and move live sts to a holder or spare yarn to return to later.

LEFT STRAP
Rejoin the yarn to WS of work.

Next row (WS): (K1, sl1wyif) 3 times. Turn. Repeat the last row until strap measures approximately 12 inches (30.5 cm), or desired length to match the right strap. Break the yarn and move live sts to a holder or spare yarn to return to later.

NOTE: Keep in mind that knit straps stretch with time, so feel free to adjust the length for your perfect fit.

BACK
Rejoin the yarn to RS of work.

Row 1 (RS): Bind off 25 (31, 37, 41, 47) (53, 57, 64, 68, 74) sts, work rem sts in patt [51 (57, 63, 67, 73) (79, 83, 90, 94, 100) sts rem].
Row 2 (WS): Bind off 25 (31, 37, 41, 47) (53, 57, 64, 68, 74) sts, work rem sts in patt until last st, sl1wyif [26 sts rem for all sizes].
Row 3: Sl2wyib, slip first st over the next st as if to bind off. Tighten gently and work in patt until last st, sl1wyif [25 sts rem for all sizes].
Row 4: Sl2wyib, slip first st over the next st as if to bind off. Tighten gently and work in patt until last st, sl1wyif [24 sts rem for all sizes].
Repeat rows 3 and 4 a total of 6 more times until 12 sts rem.

FINISHING
Flip your work inside out and line up the front and back pieces so the front left strap is aligned with the 6 leftmost sts on the back piece, and the front right strap is aligned with the rightmost sts. Use the 3-needle bind off to seam the front straps to the back.

Weave in any loose ends. Block your project using your preferred method.

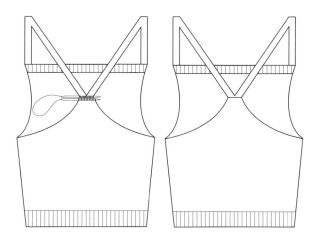

AZALEA TOP CABLE CHARTS AND LEGENDS

Chart A

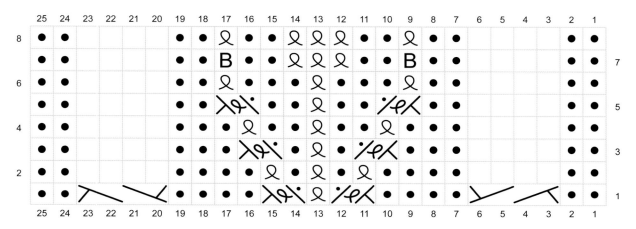

Legend A

☐	RS: K WS: P
•	RS: P WS: K
ℛ	RS: k1tbl WS: p1tbl
B	MB: (yo, k) 3 times into the next stitch. Turn work. Sl1wyif, p5. Turn work. Sl1wyib, k5. Turn work. (p2tog) 3 times. Turn work. Sl1wyib, k2tog, pass slipped st over the next st [1 st rem]
⟋℮⟍	1/1 RPT: slip 1 st to cn and hold in back, k1tbl, p1 from cn
⟍℮⟋	1/1 LPT: slip 1 st to cn and hold in front, p1, k1tbl from cn
⟍⟋	2/2 RC: slip 2 sts to cn and hold in back, k2, k2 from cn
⟋⟍	2/2 LC: slip 2 sts to cn and hold in front, k2, k2 from cn

Chart B

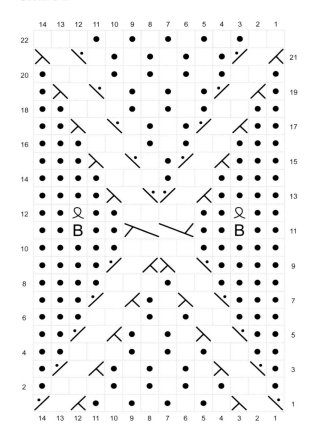

Legend B

		RS: K WS: P
	•	RS: P WS: K
	୧	RS: k1tbl WS: p1tbl
	B	MB: (yo, k) 3 times into the next stitch. Turn work. Sl1wyif, p5. Turn work. Sl1wyib, k5. Turn work. (p2tog) 3 times. Turn work. Sl1wyib, k2tog, pass slipped st over the next st [1 st rem]
⟋	⟍	2/1 RPC: slip 1 st to cn and hold in back, k2, p1 from cn
⟍	⟋	2/1 LPC: slip 2 sts to cn and hold in front, p1, k2 from cn
⟋⟍	⟍⟋	2/2 LC: slip 2 sts to cn and hold in front, k2, k2 from cn

Azalea Cardigan

A summer cardigan might sound like an oxymoron, but the lightweight nature of the Azalea Cardigan fits that description perfectly. With a plunging V-neckline held together with a tie-front closure, the Azalea Cardigan fits like a dream and is cropped for easy styling. With capped sleeves and textured cable details, this cardi is a cute and trendy addition to your handknit wardrobe. The Azalea Cardigan can be coordinated with the matching Azalea Top (page 127), a camisole, or just on its own if you're feeling a little bold and risqué. Alternatively, you can also pair the cardi with a romper or a jumpsuit for a sportier, laid-back vibe.

Construction Notes

The cardigan is worked flat in three separate panels: the front left, front right and back pieces. The panels are then seamed, stitches are picked up around the armholes and short rows are worked for the sleeves. An applied I-cord is worked along the front right panel from the bottom to the V-neck, and is then extended as one of the front ties. The applied I-cord edge continues up the right side of the V-neck, across the back neck, and down the left side of the V-neck before extending to create the other front tie, mirroring the right side. Finally, the applied I-cord edge is worked down the rest of the front left panel.

SKILL LEVEL
Intermediate

SIZING
XS (S, M, L, XL) (2XL, 3XL, 4XL, 5XL, 6XL)
29 (33.25, 37, 41, 44.75) (48.5, 53, 57.25, 61, 65.25)" / 73.75 (84.5, 94, 104.25, 113.75) (123.25, 134.5, 145.5, 155, 165.75) cm, blocked

MATERIALS
Yarn
DK weight, Stitch & Story Secret Garden in Lily White (60% Cotton, 40% Acrylic), 218 yds (200 m) per 100-g skein

Any DK weight yarn can be used for this pattern as long as it matches gauge.

Yardage/Meterage
570 (645, 690, 765, 865) (895, 985, 1050, 1105, 1290) yds / 520 (590, 630, 700, 790) (820, 900, 960, 1010, 1180) m of DK weight yarn

Needles
For ribbing and body: US 6 (4 mm), 24- to 60-inch (60- to 150-cm) circular needles
For body applied I-cord and front ties: US 4 (3.5 mm) double pointed needles
For sleeve applied I-cord: US 6 (4 mm) double pointed needles

Notions
Cable needle
Scissors
Stitch markers
Tapestry needle

GAUGE
21.5 sts x 32 rows = 4 inches (10 cm) in moss stitch worked flat using larger needles (blocked)

25 sts x 32 rows = 4 inches (10 cm) in Chart A worked flat using larger needles (blocked)

18 sts x 30 rounds = 4 inches (10 cm) in stockinette st in the round using larger needles (blocked)

TECHNIQUES
Applied I-cord Edge (explained within the pattern)
German Short Rows (page 163)
I-cord Bind Off (explained within the pattern)
Longtail Cast On (page 157)
Moss Stitch (page 162)
Vertical Invisible Seam (page 161)

ABBREVIATIONS

0 or -	no stitch / step does not apply to your size
1x1 ribbing	*k1, p1; repeat from * repeat until end
BOR	beginning of round
cn	cable needle
DPN(s)	double pointed needle(s)
DS	double stitch
k	knit
k1tbl	knit through the back loop
MDS	make double stitch [see German short rows in Techniques (page 155)]
p	purl
p1tbl	purl through the back loop
p2tog	purl 2 sts together [1 st decreased]
sl1wyib	slip 1 st purlwise with yarn in back
sl1wyif	slip 1 st purlwise with yarn in front
pm	place marker
rem	remain(ing)
RS	right side
sm	slip marker
ssk	slip 2 sts knitwise, one at a time; move both stitches back to the left needle; knit these 2 sts together through the back loops [1 st decreased]
st(s)	stitch(es)
stm	stitch marker
work(ing) even	continue working the pattern as established without any increases or decreases
WS	wrong side
yo	yarnover

Cable stitch abbreviations can be found in the Legends on pages 145–146.

SCHEMATIC

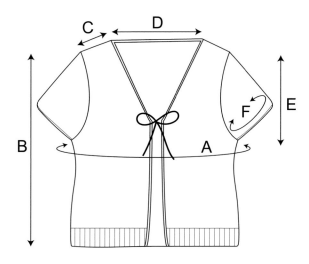

SIZING CHART

		XS	S	M	L	XL	2XL	3XL	4XL	5XL	6XL
A) Body circumference (tied)	in	29	33.25	37	41	44.75	48.5	53	57.25	61	65.25
	cm	73.75	84.5	94	104.25	113.75	123.5	134.5	145.5	155	165.75
B) Garment length	in	17	17.5	18.5	19	20	21	22	23	23.5	24.5
	cm	43.25	44.5	47	48.25	50.75	53.25	56	58.5	59.75	62.25
C) Shoulder width	in	4	5	5.5	6	6.75	7.75	8	8.75	9.25	10.5
	cm	10.25	12.75	14	15.25	17.25	19.75	20.25	22.25	23.5	26.75
D) Back neck	in	4	5	5.5	6.25	6.75	7.75	8	8.75	9.25	10.5
	cm	10.25	12.75	14	16	17.25	19.75	20.25	22.25	23.5	26.75
E) Armhole depth	in	7.5	8	8.5	9	9.5	10	10.5	11	11.5	12
	cm	19	20.25	21.5	22.75	24.25	25.5	26.75	28	29.25	30.5
F) Sleeve circumference	in	15.5	16.5	17.25	18.75	19.5	20.5	21.75	22.75	23.5	24.5
	cm	39.25	42	43.75	47.75	49.5	52	55.25	57.75	59.75	62.25

This cardigan is designed with a range of 1.5 inches (3.75 cm) of negative ease to 1.25 inches (3.25 cm) of positive ease. Sample shown is knit in size XS.

AZALEA CARDIGAN PATTERN

FRONT RIGHT

Using US 6 (4 mm) needles, cast on 45 (51, 57, 63, 69) (75, 79, 85, 91, 97) sts using the longtail cast on method.

Row 1 (RS): (K1, p1) until last st, k1.
Row 2 (WS): (P1, k1) until last st, p1.

Repeat the last 2 rows until ribbing measures 1.5 inches (3.75 cm) from the cast on edge, ending on a WS row.

Sizes XS–S only

Set-up row 1 (RS): (K1, p1) 3 times, work row 1 of Chart A (page 145), (k1, p1) 7 (10, -, -, -) (-, -, -, -, -) times.
Set-up row 2 (WS): (K1, p1) 7 (10, -, -, -) (-, -, -, -, -) times, work row 2 of Chart A, (k1, p1) 3 times.
Set-up row 3: (P1, k1) 3 times, work row 3 of Chart A, (p1, k1) 7 (10, -, -, -) (-, -, -, -, -) times.
Set-up row 4: (P1, k1) 7 (10, -, -, -) (-, -, -, -, -) times, work row 4 of Chart A, (p1, k1) 3 times.

Sizes M–2XL only

Set-up row 1 (RS): (K1, p1) 3 times, work row 1 of Chart A (page 145), work row 1 of Chart B (page 146), p2, (k1, p1) - (-, 5, 8, 11) (14, -, -, -, -) times.
Set-up row 2 (WS): (K1, p1) - (-, 5, 8, 11) (14, -, -, -, -) times, k2, work row 2 of Chart B, work row 2 of Chart A, (k1, p1) 3 times.
Set-up row 3: (P1, k1) 3 times, work row 3 of Chart A, work row 3 of Chart B, p2, (p1, k1) - (-, 5, 8, 11) (14, -, -, -, -) times.
Set-up row 4: (P1, k1) - (-, 5, 8, 11) (14, -, -, -, -) times, k2, work row 4 of Chart B, work row 4 of Chart A, (p1, k1) 3 times.

Sizes 3XL–6XL only

Set-up row 1 (RS): (K1, p1) 3 times, work row 1 of Chart A (page 145), work row 1 of Chart B (page 146), work row 1 of Chart A, p1, (k1, p1) - (-, -, -, -) (-, 4, 7, 10, 13) times.
Set-up row 2 (WS): (K1, p1) - (-, -, -, -) (-, 4, 7, 10, 13) times, k1, work row 2 of Chart A, work row 2 of Chart B, work row 2 of Chart A, (k1, p1) 3 times.
Set-up row 3: (P1, k1) 3 times, work row 3 of Chart A, work row 3 of Chart B, work row 3 of Chart A, p1, (p1, k1) - (-, -, -, -) (-, 4, 7, 10, 13) times.
Set-up row 4: (P1, k1) - (-, -, -, -) (-, 4, 7, 10, 13) times, k1, work row 4 of Chart A, work row 4 of Chart B, work row 4 of Chart A, (p1, k1) 3 times.

All Sizes Resume

Work even until the piece measures 9.5 (9.5, 10, 10, 10.5) (11, 11.5, 12, 12, 12.5) inches / 24.25 (24.25, 25.5, 25.5, 26.75) (28, 29.25, 30.5, 30.5, 31.75) cm from the cast on edge. Your last row should be a RS row.

> **NOTE:** Missed a bobble? Not to worry, you can knit one separately and sew it on afterwards. All you have to do is make a slipknot and follow the rest of the instructions for making a bobble. Break the yarn, leaving approximately a 3-inch (7.5-cm) tail. Close the stitch by threading the tail through it. Fasten the bobble into place.

Begin Decreases

Row 1 (WS, armhole decrease): Bind off 4 (4, 4, 6, 6) (6, 6, 8, 8, 8) sts, work in patt until end [41 (47, 53, 57, 63) (69, 73, 77, 83, 89) sts rem].
Row 2 (RS): Work in patt.
Row 3 (WS, armhole decrease): Bind off 1 st, work in patt until end [40 (46, 52, 56, 62) (68, 72, 76, 82, 88) sts rem].
Row 4 (RS, neckline decrease): Bind off 1 st, work in patt until end [39 (45, 51, 55, 61) (67, 71, 75, 81, 87) sts rem].

Continue binding off 1 st from the armhole edge a total of 4 (4, 6, 6, 7) (7, 8, 8, 9, 9) more times, while *at the same time* binding off 1 st from the neckline edge from the RS a total of 14 (14, 16, 16, 18) (18, 20, 20, 22, 22) more times [after all decreases, 21 (27, 29, 33, 36) (42, 43, 47, 50, 56) sts rem].

Work even until the piece measures 17 (17.5, 18.5, 19, 20) (21, 22, 23, 23.5, 24.5) inches / 43.25 (44.5, 47, 48.25, 50.75) (53.25, 56, 58.5, 59.75, 62.25) cm from the cast on edge. Your last row should be a RS row. Break the yarn and move live sts to a holder or spare yarn to return to later.

FRONT LEFT

Using US 6 (4 mm) needles, cast on 45 (51, 57, 63, 69) (75, 79, 85, 91, 97) sts using the longtail cast on method.

Row 1 (RS): (K1, p1) until last st, k1.
Row 2 (WS): (P1, k1) until last st, p1.
Repeat the last 2 rows until ribbing measures 1.5 inches (3.75 cm) from the cast on edge, ending on a WS row.

Sizes XS–S only

Set-up row 1 (RS): (K1, p1) 7 (10, -, -, -) (-, -, -, -, -) times, work row 1 of Chart A, (k1, p1) 3 times.
Set-up row 2 (WS): (K1, p1) 3 times, work row 2 of Chart A, (k1, p1) 7 (10, -, -, -) (-, -, -, -, -) times.
Set-up row 3: (P1, k1) 7 (10, -, -, -) (-, -, -, -, -) times, work row 3 of Chart A, (p1, k1) 3 times.
Set-up row 4: (P1, k1) 3 times, work row 4 of Chart A, (p1, k1) 7 (10, -, -, -) (-, -, -, -, -) times.

Sizes M–2XL only

Set-up row 1 (RS): (K1, p1) - (-, 5, 8, 11) (14, -, -, -, -) times, p2, work row 1 of Chart B, work row 1 of Chart A, (k1, p1) 3 times.
Set-up row 2 (WS): (K1, p1) 3 times, work row 2 of Chart A, work row 2 of Chart B, k2, (k1, p1) - (-, 5, 8, 11) (14, -, -, -, -) times.
Set-up row 3: (P1, k1) - (-, 5, 8, 11) (14, -, -, -, -) times, p2, work row 3 of Chart B, work row 3 of Chart A, (p1, k1) 3 times.
Set-up row 4: (P1, k1) 3 times, work row 4 of Chart A, work row 4 of Chart B, k2, (p1, k1) - (-, 5, 8, 11) (14, -, -, -, -) times.

Sizes 3XL–6XL only

Set-up row 1 (RS): (K1, p1) - (-, -, -, -) (-, 4, 7, 10, 13) times, p1, work row 1 of Chart A, work row 1 of Chart B, work row 1 of Chart A, (k1, p1) 3 times.

Set-up row 2 (WS): (K1, p1) 3 times, work row 2 of Chart A, work row 2 of Chart B, work row 2 of Chart A, k1, (k1, p1) - (-, -, -, -) (-, 4, 7, 10, 13) times.

Set-up row 3: (P1, k1) - (-, -, -, -) (-, 4, 7, 10, 13) times, p1, work row 3 of Chart A, work row 3 of Chart B, work row 3 of Chart A, (p1, k1) 3 times.

Set-up row 4: (P1, k1) 3 times, work row 4 of Chart A, work row 4 of Chart B, work row 4 of Chart A, k1, (p1, k1) - (-, -, -, -) (-, 4, 7, 10, 13) times.

All Sizes Resume

Work even until the piece measures 9.5 (9.5, 10, 10, 10.5) (11, 11.5, 12, 12, 12.5) inches / 24.25 (24.25, 25.5, 25.5, 26.75) (28, 29.25, 30.5, 30.5, 31.75) cm from the cast on edge. Your last row should be a WS row.

Begin Decreases

Row 1 (RS, armhole decrease): Bind off 4 (4, 4, 6, 6) (6, 6, 8, 8, 8) sts, work in patt until end [41 (47, 53, 57, 63) (69, 73, 77, 83, 89) sts rem].

Row 2 (WS): Work in patt.

Row 3 (RS, armhole decrease): Bind off 1 st, work in patt until end [40 (46, 52, 56, 62) (68, 72, 76, 82, 88) sts rem].

Row 4 (WS, neckline decrease): Bind off 1 st, work in patt until end [39 (45, 51, 55, 61) (67, 71, 75, 81, 87) sts rem].

Continue binding off 1 st from the armhole edge a total of 4 (4, 6, 6, 7) (7, 8, 8, 9, 9) more times, while *at the same time* binding off 1 st from the neckline edge a total of 14 (14, 16, 16, 18) (18, 20, 20, 22, 22) more times [after all decreases, 21 (27, 29, 33, 36) (42, 43, 47, 50, 56) sts rem].

Work even until the piece measures 17 (17.5, 18.5, 19, 20) (21, 22, 23, 23.5, 24.5) inches / 43.25 (44.5, 47, 48.25, 50.75) (53.25, 56, 58.5, 59.75, 62.25) cm from the cast on edge. Your last row should be a RS row. Break the yarn and move live sts to a holder or spare yarn to return to later.

BACK

Using US 6 (4 mm) needles, cast on 92 (104, 116, 128, 140) (152, 160, 172, 184, 196) sts using the longtail cast on method.

Work in 1x1 ribbing for 1.5 inches (3.75 cm), ending on a WS row.

Sizes XS–S only

Set-up row 1 (RS): (K1, p1) 7 (10, -, -, -) (-, -, -, -, -) times, work row 1 of Chart A, work row 1 of Chart B, work row 1 of Chart A, (k1, p1) 7 (10, -, -, -) (-, -, -, -, -) times.

Set-up row 2 (WS): (K1, p1) 7 (10, -, -, -) (-, -, -, -, -) times, work row 2 of Chart A, work row 2 of Chart B, work row 2 of Chart A, (k1, p1) 7 (10, -, -, -) (-, -, -, -, -) times.

Set-up row 3: (P1, k1) 7 (10, -, -, -) (-, -, -, -, -) times, work row 3 of Chart A, work row 3 of Chart B, work row 3 of Chart A, (p1, k1) 7 (10, -, -, -) (-, -, -, -, -) times.

Set-up row 4: (P1, k1) 7 (10, -, -, -) (-, -, -, -, -) times, work row 4 of Chart A, work row 4 of Chart B, work row 4 of Chart A, (p1, k1) 7 (10, -, -, -) (-, -, -, -, -) times.

Sizes M–2XL only

Set-up row 1 (RS): (K1, p1) - (-, 5, 8, 11) (14, -, -, -, -) times, p2, work row 1 of Chart B, work row 1 of Chart A, work row 1 of Chart B, work row 1 of Chart A, work row 1 of Chart B, p2, (k1, p1) - (-, 5, 8, 11) (14, -, -, -, -) times.

Set-up row 2 (WS): (K1, p1) - (-, 5, 8, 11) (14, -, -, -, -) times, k2, work row 2 of Chart B, work row 2 of Chart A, work row 2 of Chart B, work row 2 of Chart A, work row 2 of Chart B, k2, (k1, p1) - (-, 5, 8, 11) (14, -, -, -, -) times.

Set-up row 3: (P1, k1) - (-, 5, 8, 11) (14, -, -, -, -) times, p2, work row 3 of Chart B, work row 3 of Chart A, work row 3 of Chart B, work row 3 of Chart A, work row 3 of Chart B, p2, (p1, k1) - (-, 5, 8, 11) (14, -, -, -, -) times.

Set-up row 4: (P1, k1) - (-, 5, 8, 11) (14, -, -, -, -) times, k2, work row 4 of Chart B, work row 4 of Chart A, work row 4 of Chart B, work row 2 of Chart A, work row 4 of Chart B, k2, (p1, k1) - (-, 5, 8, 11) (14, -, -, -, -) times.

Sizes 3XL–6XL only

Set-up row 1 (RS): (K1, p1) - (-, -, -, -) (-, 4, 7, 10, 13) times, p1, work row 1 of Chart A, work row 1 of Chart B, work row 1 of Chart A, work row 1 of Chart B, work row 1 of Chart A, work row 1 of Chart B, work row 1 of Chart A, p1, (k1, p1) - (-, -, -, -) (-, 4, 7, 10, 13) times.

Set-up row 2 (WS): (K1, p1) - (-, -, -, -) (-, 4, 7, 10, 13) times, k1, work row 2 of Chart A, work row 2 of Chart B, work row 2 of Chart A, work row 2 of Chart B, work row 2 of Chart A, work row 2 of Chart B, work row 2 of Chart A, k1, (k1, p1) - (-, -, -, -) (-, 4, 7, 10, 13) times.

Set-up row 3: (P1, k1) - (-, -, -, -) (-, 4, 7, 10, 13) times, p1, work row 3 of Chart A, work row 3 of Chart B, work row 3 of Chart A, work row 3 of Chart B, work row 3 of Chart A, work row 3 of Chart B, work row 3 of Chart A, p1, (p1, k1) - (-, -, -, -) (-, 4, 7, 10, 13) times.

Set-up row 4: (P1, k1) - (-, -, -, -) (-, 4, 7, 10, 13) times, k1, work row 4 of Chart A, work row 4 of Chart B, work row 4 of Chart A, work row 4 of Chart B, work row 4 of Chart A, work row 4 of Chart B, work row 4 of Chart A, k1, (p1, k1) - (-, -, -, -) (-, 4, 7, 10, 13) times.

All Sizes Resume

Work even until the piece measures 9.5 (9.5, 10, 10, 10.5) (11, 11.5, 12, 12, 12.5) inches / 24.25 (24.25, 25.5, 25.5, 26.75) (28, 29.25, 30.5, 30.5, 31.75) cm from the cast on edge. Your last row should be a WS row.

Begin Armhole Decreases

Row 1 (RS): Bind off 4 (4, 6, 6, 7) (7, 8, 8, 9, 9) sts, work in patt until end [88 (100, 110, 122, 133) (145, 152, 164, 175, 187) sts rem].

Row 2 (WS): Bind off 4 (4, 6, 6, 7) (7, 8, 8, 9, 9) sts, work in patt until end [84 (96, 104, 116, 126) (138, 144, 156, 166, 178) sts rem].

Row 3: Bind off 1 st, work in patt until end [83 (95, 103, 115, 125) (137, 143, 155, 165, 177) sts rem].

Row 4: Bind off 1 st, work in patt until end [82 (94, 102, 114, 124) (136, 142, 154, 164, 176) sts rem].

Repeat the last 2 rows 4 (4, 4, 6, 6) (6, 6, 8, 8, 8) more times [74 (86, 94, 102, 112) (124, 130, 138, 148, 160) sts rem].

Work even until the piece measures 5 rows before the last row on the front pieces [approximately 16.5 (17, 18, 18.5, 19.5) (20.5, 21.5, 22.5, 23, 24) inches / 42 (43.25, 45.75, 47, 49.5) (52, 54.5, 57.25, 58.5, 61) cm from the cast on edge]. Your last row should be a WS row.

Next row (RS): Work 23 (29, 31, 35, 38) (44, 45, 49, 52, 58) sts in patt, bind off 28 (28, 32, 32, 36) (36, 40, 40, 44, 44) sts, work rem 23 (29, 31, 35, 38) (44, 45, 49, 52, 58) sts in patt. Turn and leave back right shoulder sts on a holder or spare yarn to return to later.

TIP: Mark where you left off in the charts.

BACK LEFT SHOULDER

Row 1 (WS): Work in patt.
Row 2 (RS): Bind off 1 st, work in patt until end [22 (28, 30, 34, 37) (43, 44, 48, 51, 57) sts rem].
Repeat rows 1 and 2 one more time [21 (27, 29, 33, 36) (42, 43, 47, 50, 56) sts rem].
Do not break the yarn. Flip work so the RSs are facing out and place your front left live sts on another US 6 (4 mm) needle. Use the 3-needle bind off method to bind off the left shoulder.

BACK RIGHT SHOULDER

Rejoin the yarn to WS of work.
Row 1 (WS): Bind off 1 st, work in patt until end [22 (28, 30, 34, 37) (43, 44, 48, 51, 57) sts rem].
Row 2 (RS): Work in patt.
Repeat rows 1 and 2 one more time [21 (27, 29, 33, 36) (42, 43, 47, 50, 56) sts rem].
Do not break the yarn. Flip work so the RSs are facing out and place your front right live sts on another US 6 (4 mm) needle. Use the 3-needle bind off method to bind off the right shoulder.

SEAMING THE BODY

Flip work so the RSs are facing out. Use the vertical invisible seaming technique to seam the sides, beginning with the cast on edge up until the bind off edge of the underarm.

APPLIED I-CORD EDGE AND TIES

Using US 4 (3.5 mm) DPNs, cast on 2 sts using the longtail cast on method. Pick up and k1 from the bottom edge of the front right panel. Slide the 3 sts down to the other end of the needle.

Next row: K1, ssk, pick up and k1 from the edge. Slide sts down to the other end of the needle. Repeat the last row, picking up 3 out of every 4 edge sts until 1 st rem before the V-neck edge.

Next row: K1, ssk. Slide sts down to the other end of the needle.

Next row: K2. Slide sts down to the other end of the needle.
Repeat the last row, continuing the I-cord front tie across 2 sts until the tie measures 13 inches (33 cm), or desired length. Bind off.

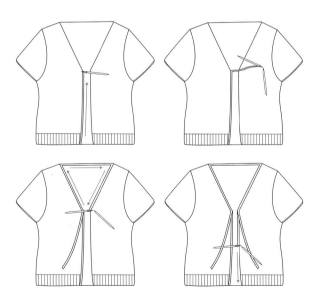

Return yarn to the bottom of the front right V-neck edge. Pick up and k3 from the edge. Slide sts down to the other end of the needle.

Next row: K1, ssk, pick up and k1 from the edge. Slide sts down to the other end of the needle. Repeat the last row, picking up 3 out every 4 edge sts until 1 st rem before the front left V-neck edge.

Next row: K1, ssk. Slide sts down to the other end of the needle.

Next row: K2. Slide sts down to the other end of the needle.
Repeat the last row, continuing the I-cord front tie across 2 sts until the tie measures 13 inches (33 cm), or until it matches the other tie. Bind off.

Return the yarn to the bottom of the front left V-neck edge. Pick up and k3 from the edge. Slide sts down to the other end of the needle.

Next row: K1, ssk, pick up and k1 from the edge. Slide sts down to the other end of the needle. Repeat the last row, picking up 3 out of every 4 edge sts until you reach the last edge st of the front left panel. Bind off and weave in any loose ends.

SLEEVES (MAKE 2)
Using US 6 (4 mm) needles and beginning with the center of the underarm, pick up and k4 (4, 4, 6, 6) (6, 6, 8, 8, 8) from the bind off sts, evenly pick up and k31 (33, 35, 36, 38) (40, 43, 43, 45, 47) towards the shoulder, pm, evenly pick up and k31 (33, 35, 36, 38) (40, 43, 43, 45, 47) back towards the underarm, and pick up and k4 (4, 4, 6, 6) (6, 6, 8, 8, 8) from the underarm bind off sts. Pm and join for working in the round [70 (74, 78, 84, 88) (92, 98, 102, 106, 110) sts].

Short Row Shaping
Short row 1 (RS): K until stm, sm, k4, turn.
Short row 2 (WS): MDS, p until stm, sm, p4, turn.
Short row 3: MDS, k until stm, sm, k until 4 sts past DS (resolving existing DS), turn.
Short row 4: MDS, p until stm, sm, p until 4 sts past DS (resolving existing DS), turn.
Repeat the last 2 rows 5 (5, 5, 7, 7) (7, 7, 9, 9, 9) more times. In your final row, turn your work. MDS, k until shoulder stm, remove marker, and continue in patt until BOR stm, resolving DS along the way. You will be working in the round for the remainder of the sleeve.

K all rounds, resolving the final DS along the way, until the sleeve measures 2.5 inches (6.5 cm) from the armhole edge, or until it reaches desired length. Remove BOR stm.

I-cord Sleeve Bind Off
Using a US 6 (4 mm) DPN as your right-hand needle, insert it between the first and second stitch of your left-hand needle. Wrap working yarn around your needle and draw it up so you have a new stitch. Place the new stitch onto the left-hand needle. Repeat one more time so you have a total of two new stitches.

Next step: K1, ssk from the left needle. Move the 2 sts back to the left-hand needle.

Repeat the last step until no sleeve sts rem. Bind off and seam the ends of the I-cord together.

FINISHING
Weave in any loose ends, ensuring the gaps between the front I-cord ties and the V-neck edge are closed. Block your project using your preferred method.

AZALEA CARDIGAN CABLE CHARTS AND LEGENDS

Chart A

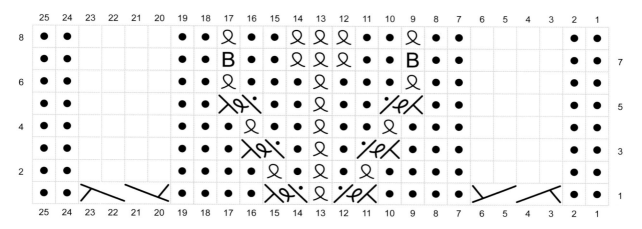

Legend A

☐	RS: K WS: P
•	RS: P WS: K
Ω	RS: k1tbl WS: p1tbl
B	MB: (yo, k) 3 times into the next stitch. Turn work. Sl1wyif, p5. Turn work. Sl1wyib, k5. Turn work. (p2tog) 3 times. Turn work. Sl1wyib, k2tog, pass slipped st over the next st [1 st rem]
⟋⊘⟍	1/1 RPT: slip 1 st to cn and hold in back, k1tbl, p1 from cn
⟍⊘⟋	1/1 LPT: slip 1 st to cn and hold in front, p1, k1tbl from cn
⟍⟋	2/2 RC: slip 2 sts to cn and hold in back, k2, k2 from cn
⟋⟍	2/2 LC: slip 2 sts to cn and hold in front, k2, k2 from cn

Chart B

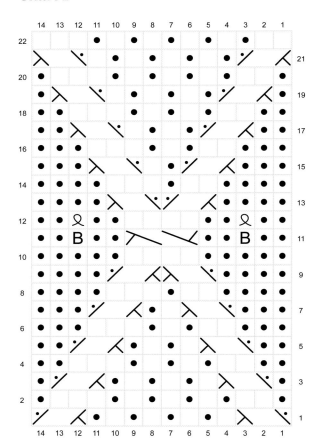

Legend B

	☐	RS: K WS: P
	•	RS: P WS: K
	Omega	RS: k1tbl WS: p1tbl
	B	MB: (yo, k) 3 times into the next stitch. Turn work. Sl1wyif, p5. Turn work. Sl1wyib, k5. Turn work. (p2tog) 3 times. Turn work. Sl1wyib, k2tog, pass slipped st over the next st [1 st rem]
╱	╲	2/1 RPC: slip 1 st to cn and hold in back, k2, p1 from cn
╲	╱	2/1 LPC: slip 2 sts to cn and hold in front, p1, k2 from cn
╲	╲	2/2 LC: slip 2 sts to cn and hold in front, k2, k2 from cn

Rosemary Sweater

The Rosemary Sweater is a cabled mohair dream. Boxy with slim sleeves, the sweater has an all-around cable-and-lace pattern that incorporates classic elements into a modern shape. The body begins and ends with a twisted rib, providing symmetry in both directions by creating a clean and simple boatneck finish that draws the eye out towards the shoulders. Knit with two strands of lace mohair yarn held throughout, the result is an airy, slightly sheer fabric with exceptional drape. The wide neckline and open fabric mean extra versatility: You can style the sweater over a lacy bralette or even a camisole. The sweater is also perfect over a slip dress for a sleek and sophisticated look that can be worn year-round. The sleeves can also be left off as a warmer weather alternative.

Construction Notes

The sweater is worked flat from the bottom up in identical panels, beginning and ending with a twisted rib. Once both panels are complete, the shoulders and sides are seamed. Because the sweater is finished with seaming, you are able to customize the width of the neck opening as well as the sleeves (for example, you can knit a size XS body and size M sleeves). Keep in mind that if you decide to customize your sweater, you will need a different amount of yarn than what is listed in the pattern. Stitches are picked up around the armhole and the sleeves are worked from the top down. There is no additional finishing needed for the neckline due to the twisted rib edge.

SKILL LEVEL
Intermediate

SIZING
XS (S, M, L, XL) (2XL, 3XL, 4XL, 5XL, 6XL)
44.5 (47.75, 52, 56, 59.25) (63.75, 67.75, 72, 76, 79.25)" / 113 (121.25, 132, 142.25, 150.5) (162, 172, 183, 193, 201.25) cm, blocked

MATERIALS
Yarn
Lace weight (held double), DROPS Kid-Silk in 9 (75% Mohair, 25% Silk), 230 yds (210 m) per 25-g skein

Any lace weight yarn held double can be used for this pattern as long as it matches gauge.

Yardage/Meterage
1800 (1910, 2090, 2400, 2565) (2615, 2740, 2920, 3080, 3220) yds / 1650 (1750, 1915, 2200, 2350) (2395, 2510, 2675, 2825, 2950) m of lace weight yarn

Needles
For ribbing: US 6 (4 mm), 24- to 60-inch (60- to 150-cm) circular needles
For body: US 8 (5 mm), 24- to 60-inch (60- to 150-cm) circular needles
For sleeves: US 8 (5 mm), double pointed needles
For sleeve ribbing: US 6 (4 mm), double pointed needles

Notions
Cable needle
Scissors
Stitch marker(s)
Tapestry needle

GAUGE
20 sts x 28 rounds/rows = 4 inches (10 cm) in stockinette st worked both flat and in the round using larger needles (blocked)

22 sts x 28 rounds/rows = 4 inches (10 cm) in Charts A or D worked both flat and in the round using larger needles (blocked)

TECHNIQUES
Horizontal Invisible Seam (page 161)
Longtail Cast On (page 157)
Vertical Invisible Seam (page 161)

ABBREVIATIONS

0 or -	no stitch / step does not apply to your size
1x1 ribbing	*k1, p1; repeat from * until end
1x1 twisted ribbing	*k1tbl, p1tbl; repeat from * until end
cn	cable needle
DPN(s)	double pointed needle(s)
k	knit
k1tbl	knit through the back loop
k2tog	knit 2 sts together [1 st decreased]
RS	right side
p	purl
p1tbl	purl through the back loop
patt	pattern
pm	place marker
rem	remain(ing)
ssk	slip 2 sts knitwise, one at a time; move both stitches back to the left needle; knit these 2 sts together through the back loops [1 st decreased]
st(s)	stitch(es)
WS	wrong side
yo	yarnover

Cable stitch abbreviations can be found in the Legends on pages 152 and 154.

SCHEMATIC

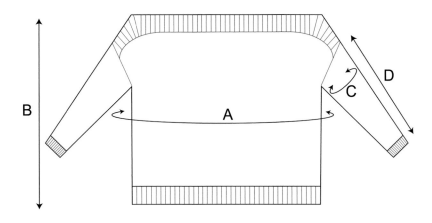

SIZING CHART

		XS	S	M	L	XL	2XL	3XL	4XL	5XL	6XL
A) Body circumference	in	44.5	47.75	52	56	59.25	63.75	67.75	72	76	79.25
	cm	113	121.25	132	142.25	150.5	162	172	183	193	201.25
B) Garment length	in	18.25	18.75	19.25	19.75	20.25	20.75	21.25	21.75	22.25	22.75
	cm	46.25	47.75	49	50.25	51.5	52.75	54	55.25	56.5	57.75
C) Sleeve circumference	in	10.75	11.5	12.25	13.25	14.5	16.5	18.25	19	19.5	20.25
	cm	27.25	29.25	31	33.75	36.75	42	46.25	48.25	49.5	51.5
D) Sleeve length	in	16.25	16.25	16.75	17.25	17.25	17.75	18.25	18.25	18.75	19.25
	cm	41.25	41.25	42.5	43.75	43.75	45	46.25	46.25	47.75	49

This sweater is designed with 13–16 inches (33–40.75 cm) of positive ease. Sample shown is knit in size XS. If you are between sizes, select the smaller size.

ROSEMARY SWEATER PATTERN

BODY PANELS (MAKE 2)

Using US 6 (4 mm) needles and two strands held together, cast on 132 (140, 152, 162, 170) (182, 192, 204, 214, 222) sts using the longtail cast on method.

Work in 1x1 twisted ribbing for 1.5 inches (3.75 cm).

Switch to US 8 (5 mm) needles.

Next row (WS): P all sts.

Set-up row 1 (RS): *K5 (9, 2, 7, 11) (4, 9, 2, 7, 11), work row 1 of Chart A (page 152) 2 (2, 3, 3, 3) (4, 4, 5, 5, 5) times, work row 1 of Chart B (page 153), work row 1 of Chart C (page 153), work row 1 of Chart B, work row 1 of Chart D (page 154) 2 (2, 3, 3, 3) (4, 4, 5, 5, 5) times, k5 (9, 2, 7, 11) (4, 9, 2, 7, 11).

Set-up row 2 (WS): *P5 (9, 2, 7, 11) (4, 9, 2, 7, 11), work row 2 of Chart D 2 (2, 3, 3, 3) (4, 4, 5, 5, 5) times, work row 2 of Chart B, work row 2 of Chart C, work row 2 of Chart B, work row 2 of Chart A 2 (2, 3, 3, 3) (4, 4, 5, 5, 5) times, p5 (9, 2, 7, 11) (4, 9, 2, 7, 11).

NOTE: Place stitch markers between cable charts to better keep track of your work and to differentiate the cable patterns more easily.

Continue working in patt as established until the piece measures 16.5 (17, 17.5, 18, 18.5) (19, 19.5, 20, 20.5, 21) inches / 42 (43.25, 44.5, 45.75, 47) (48.25, 49.5, 50.75, 52, 53.25) cm from the cast on edge. Your last row should be a RS row.

Switch to US 6 (4 mm) needles.

Next row (WS): P all sts.

Work in 1x1 twisted ribbing for 1.75 inches (4.5 cm). Your last row should be a RS row.

Work one row in regular 1x1 ribbing. Bind off all sts knitwise through the back loop.

SEAMING THE BODY

With the RSs facing out, use the invisible horizontal seaming method and seam the shoulders, leaving a 10-inch (25.5-cm) neck opening, or your desired width.

If you are mixing and matching sizes, switch to your chosen sleeve size here. Use the vertical invisible seaming technique to seam the sides, leaving a 6.5 (7, 7.5, 8, 8.5) (9.5, 9.5, 10, 10.5, 11)-inch / 16.5 (17.75, 19, 20.25, 21.5) (24.25, 24.25, 25.5, 26.75, 28)-cm gap for the sleeve opening.

SLEEVES (MAKE 2)

Using US 8 (5 mm) circular needles or DPNs and two strands held together, beginning with the center of the underarm, evenly pick up and k32 (34, 36, 38, 42) (47, 51, 53, 55, 57) towards the shoulder, then evenly pick up and k32 (34, 36, 38, 42) (47, 51, 53, 55, 57) back towards the underarm. Pm and join for working in the round [64 (68, 72, 76, 84) (94, 102, 106, 110, 114) sts].

Round 1: K5 (7, 9, 11, 2) (7, 11, 13, 2, 4), work round 1 of Chart A 1 (1, 1, 1, 2) (2, 2, 2, 3, 3) time(s), p2, work round 1 of Chart C, p2, work round 1 of Chart D 1 (1, 1, 1, 2) (2, 2, 2, 3, 3) time(s), k5 (7, 9, 11, 2) (7, 11, 13, 2, 4).
Round 2: K5 (7, 9, 11, 2) (7, 11, 13, 2, 4), work round 2 of Chart A 1 (1, 1, 1, 2) (2, 2, 2, 3, 3) time(s), p2, work round 2 of Chart C, p2, work round 2 of Chart D 1 (1, 1, 1, 2) (2, 2, 2, 3, 3) time(s), k5 (7, 9, 11, 2) (7, 11, 13, 2, 4).

Continue working in patt as established until the sleeve measures 7.5 (6.5, 6.5, 6, 6) (5, 5, 4.5, 4, 3.5) inches / 19 (16.5, 16.5, 15.25, 15.25) (12.75, 12.75, 11.5, 10.25, 9) cm from the pick up edge, or until it reaches desired length.

Decrease round: K1, k2tog, work in patt until last 3 sts, ssk, k1 [62 (66, 70, 74, 82) (92, 100, 104, 108, 112) sts rem].

Sizes XS–M only

Repeat decrease round every 8th round 4 (4, 4, -, -) (-, -, -, -, -) times, followed by every 6th round - (2, 4, -, -) (-, -, -, -, -) times [54 (54, 54, -, -) (-, -, -, -, -) sts rem].

Sizes L–6XL only

Repeat decrease round every 5th round - (-, -, 4, 7) (7, 5, 7, 6, 9) times, then every 4th round - (-, -, 6, 6) (7, 7, 9, 8, 10) times, and then every 3rd round - (-, -, -, -) (4, 9, 7, 11, 7) times [- (-, -, 54, 56) (56, 58, 58, 58, 60) sts rem].

NOTE: If you reach a point where there are not enough sts to complete a cable pattern because of the decreases, k the remaining sts instead.

All Sizes Resume

Continue working in patt as established until the sleeve measures 15 (15, 15.5, 16, 16) (16.5, 17, 17, 17.5, 18) inches / 38 (38, 39.25, 40.75, 40.75) (42, 43.25, 43.25, 44.5, 45.75) cm from the pick up edge.

Switch to US 6 (4 mm) circular needles or DPNs.

K one round.

Work in 1x1 twisted ribbing for 1.25 inches (3.25 cm). Bind off knitwise through the back loop.

FINISHING

Weave in any loose ends. Block your project using your preferred method.

ROSEMARY SWEATER CABLE CHARTS AND LEGENDS

Chart A

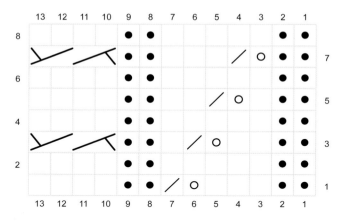

Legend A

☐	RS: K WS: P
•	RS: P WS: K
/	k2tog
○	yo
⟍⟋⟍	2/2 RC: slip 2 sts to cn and hold in back, k2, k2 from cn

Legend B

☐	RS: K WS: P
•	RS: P WS: K
/	k2tog
○	yo
⟋ ⟍	2/1 RPC: slip 1 st to cn and hold in back, k2, p1 from cn
⟍ ⟋	2/1 LPC: slip 2 sts to cn and hold in front, p1, k2 from cn

Chart B

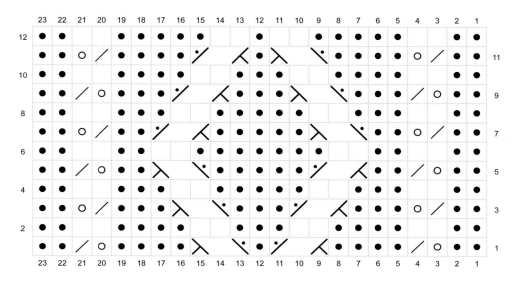

Chart C

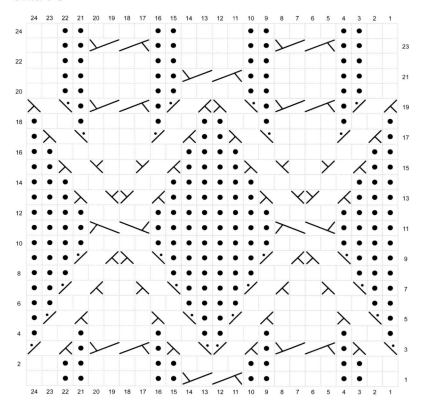

Legend C

☐	RS: K WS: P
●	RS: P WS: K
⟋ ⟍	2/1 RPC: slip 1 st to cn and hold in back, k2, p1 from cn
⟍ ⟋	2/1 LPC: slip 2 sts to cn and hold in front, p1, k2 from cn
⟋ ⟍	2/1 RC: slip 1 st to cn and hold in back, k2, k1 from cn
⟍ ⟍	2/1 LC: slip 2 sts to cn and hold in front, k1, k2 from cn
⟍⟋ ⟋⟍	2/2 RC: slip 2 sts to cn and hold in back, k2, k2 from cn
⟋⟍ ⟍⟋	2/2 LC: slip 2 sts to cn and hold in front, k2, k2 from cn

Chart D

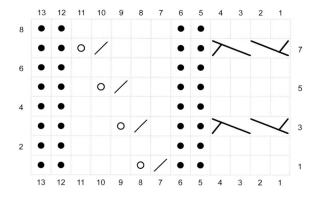

Legend D

☐	RS: K WS: P
●	RS: P WS: K
⟋	k2tog
○	yo
⟋⟍ ⟍⟋	2/2 LC: slip 2 sts to cn and hold in front, k2, k2 from cn

Techniques

In this section, you'll find tutorials on how to approach some of the most common techniques used in this book. While these are my go-to methods, there are often multiple ways to achieve the same outcome. Feel free to defer to your personal preference!

CASTING ON
Backwards Loop Cast On

The backwards loop cast on is one of the simplest cast on methods for a quick and stretchy fabric edge. It is a good method to use when casting on mid-row or round, or at the end of a row or round.

Step 1: Make a slipknot on the right needle. If casting on in an existing project, this step is not necessary.
Step 2: Wind the working yarn around your left thumb in a counterclockwise motion.
Step 3: Insert the right needle into the loop through the base of your thumb and over the yarn at the top of your thumb.
Step 4: Tighten the stitch by pulling on the working yarn.

Repeat steps 2–4 until all the stitches are cast on.

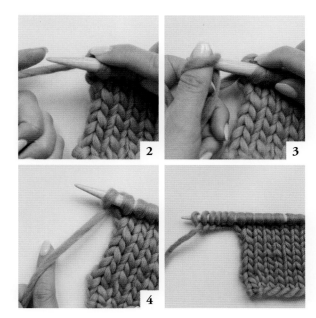

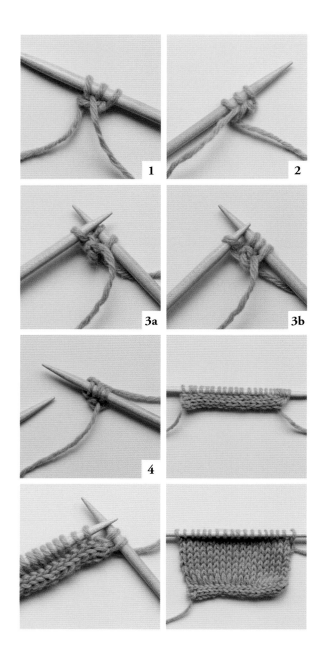

I-cord Cast On

The I-cord cast on creates a clean, rounded edge at the beginning of a project.

Step 1: Cast on 3 stitches using your preferred method.

Step 2: Slip the 3 stitches over to your left needle. Do not turn your work. The working yarn should be coming from the last stitch rather than the first stitch.

Step 3: Pull the working yarn across the back of the cast on stitches. Knit 2 stitches. Knit through the front and back of the third stitch. You should have a total of 4 stitches on your right needle.

Step 4: Slip all 4 stitches from your right needle to your left needle.

Repeat steps 3 and 4 until all the stitches are cast on, plus 3 additional stitches for finishing (for example, if your pattern calls for you to cast on 164 stitches, ensure you have 167 stitches before you move forward with the pattern). With each repeat, one stitch is added to your left needle. Once completed, slip the 4 stitches from your right needle to your left needle. K2tog twice. Slip the 2 stitches back to the left needle, then k2tog.

Longtail Cast On

The longtail cast on method is one of the most frequently used methods. It creates a firm yet elastic edge.

Step 1: Make a slipknot on the right needle. Wind the tail around your left thumb. Wrap the working yarn over your left index finger. Secure the ends in your palm for leverage.

Step 2: Insert the right needle upwards in the loop on your thumb. With the same needle, draw the working yarn through the loop to form a stitch.

Step 3: Take your thumb out of the loop and tighten the loop on the needle. Rewrap the tail around your left thumb.

Repeat steps 2 and 3 until all the stitches are cast on.

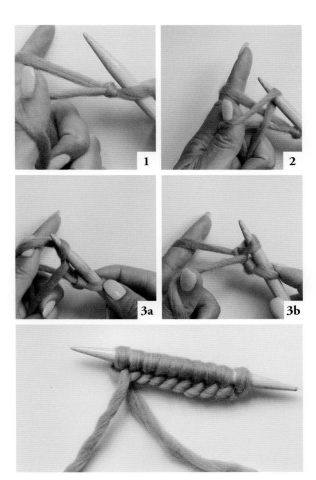

Provisional Cast On (Crochet Chain Method)

A provisional cast on temporarily holds onto live stitches to be returned to later. There are multiple approaches to this technique. This book will explore the crochet method using a locking stitch marker and a crochet hook the same size or slightly larger than your intended knitting needle. Feel free to use your preferred method for the patterns in this book.

With the crochet chain method, you will pick up and knit stitches into the back of a crochet chain with the working yarn, resulting in a completed row of stitches. Once the pattern calls for you to remove the provisional cast on, you will simply remove the locking stitch marker and pull on the tail end of the crochet chain, releasing the live stitches.

Before you begin, refer to your pattern for the number of cast on stitches required. It is recommended to chain additional stitches so you don't accidentally miss one (for example, if the pattern calls for casting on 40 stitches, chain 45 stitches).

Step 1: Using contrasting waste yarn, make a slipknot and place it on the crochet hook.
Step 2: Using your left hand to hold and steady the working yarn, loop the working yarn over the hook from back to front.
Step 3: Rotate your crochet hook, pulling the working yarn down and through the current loop on the hook.
Step 4: Repeat steps 2 and 3 until you have your desired number of chain stitches. When completed, remove the hook and clip the locking stitch marker into the final chain to keep the chain from unraveling. Break the waste yarn.
Step 5: Use your project yarn and needle to knit into the back of this crochet chain. Continue until the remainder of your stitches are cast on.

Continue with the pattern as instructed. Once you are ready to use these live stitches, remove the locking stitch marker. Gently pull on that end of the contrasting yarn and move the live stitches over one by one to your working needle until all the stitches are on your needle.

BINDING OFF
3-Needle Bind Off

This bind off is used to join two edges that have the same number of stitches. This is most commonly used to join live shoulder edges that have been placed on holders. You will need three needles for this technique, hence the name.

Step 1: Flip your work inside out so the right sides of the two pieces are facing each other and the needles are parallel.

Step 2: Insert a third needle knitwise into the first stitch of each needle and wrap the yarn around the needle as if to knit.

Step 3: Knit these two stitches together and slip them off the needle.

Step 4: Knit the next two stitches together in the same way as shown in steps 1–3.

Step 5: Slip the first stitch on the third needle over the second stitch and off the needle.

Repeat steps 4 and 5 until all the stitches are bound off.

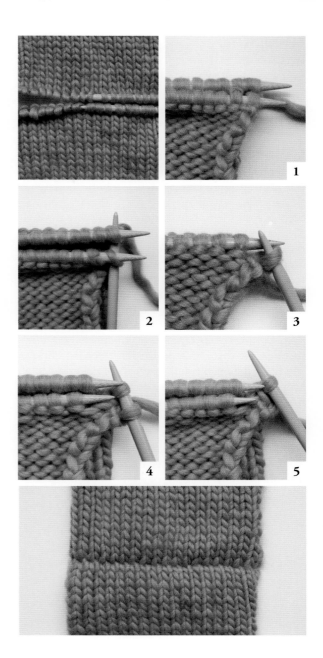

SEAMING
Kitchener Stitch

This technique is used to graft two pieces of live stitches together. Position your work so the wrong sides of the two pieces are facing each other and the needles are parallel.

Step 1: Insert your tapestry needle purlwise through the first stitch on the front needle. Pull the yarn through, leaving that stitch on the knitting needle.

Step 2: Insert your tapestry needle knitwise through the first stitch on the back needle. Pull the yarn though, leaving the stitch on the knitting needle.

Step 3: Insert your tapestry needle knitwise through the first stitch on the front needle, slip the stitch off the needle, and insert the tapestry needle purlwise through the next stitch on the front needle. Pull the yarn through, leaving this stitch on the needle.

Step 4: Insert your tapestry needle purlwise through the first stitch on the back needle. Slip the stitch off the needle and insert the tapestry needle knitwise through the next stitch on the back needle. Pull the yarn through, leaving this stitch on the needle.

Repeat steps 3 and 4 until all stitches on both the front and back needles have been grafted. Fasten off and weave in the ends.

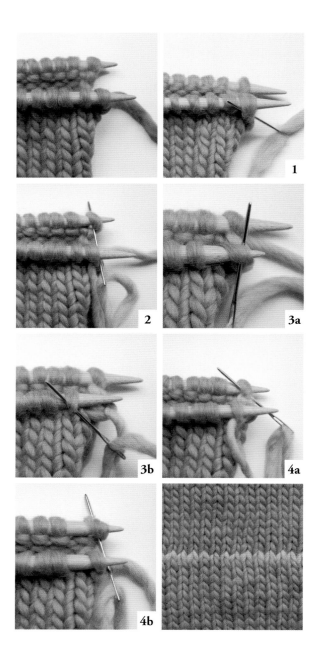

Horizontal Invisible Seam

This seaming technique is used to join two bound-off edges, most commonly for shoulder seams. In order to work this seam, you will need a tapestry needle and yarn. The recommended amount of yarn is approximately three times the length of the edge.

Step 1: Position your work so that the bound-off edges are together and lined up stitch for stitch. Thread your tapestry needle with your working yarn.

Step 2: Insert your tapestry needle under and out through the center of the first V stitch of one piece. Pull the yarn through.

Step 3: Insert your tapestry needle under the corresponding V stitch on the other piece and pull the yarn through.

Repeat steps 2 and 3 until the seam is complete.

Vertical Invisible Seam

This seaming technique is used to join two edges and is most commonly used for side seams. In order to work this seam, you will need a tapestry needle and yarn. The recommended amount of yarn is approximately 3 times the length of the edge.

Step 1: Position your work so that the right side is facing you, and the edges are lined up side by side. Thread your tapestry needle with your working yarn.

Step 2: Insert your tapestry needle under the first edge running stitch of one piece, the bar between the Vs, and pull the yarn through.

Step 3: Insert your tapestry needle under the corresponding running stitch on the other piece and pull the yarn through. Gently pull on your working yarn to bring the seams neatly together. Avoid pulling too hard as that will result in bunching of the fabric.

Repeat steps 2 and 3 until the seam is complete.

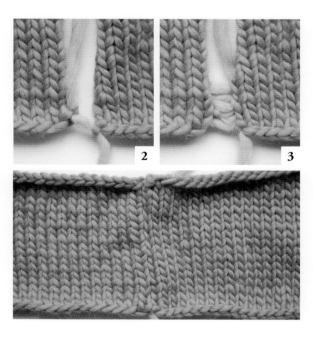

Whip Stitch

This seaming technique is used to join two edges together. It is not an invisible seam, so it is typically used in folded hems where the edge is hidden.

Step 1: Position your work so the right side is facing you. Thread your tapestry needle with your working yarn.
Step 2: Insert your tapestry needle from back to front along the edge of the right side of both pieces. Insert the needle from back to front through the next edge stitch. Pull the yarn through, allowing the yarn to wrap over the top edge.

Repeat the last step until the seam is complete.

SPECIAL STITCHES
Moss Stitch

Moss stitch is a stitch pattern made by alternating knits and purls every stitch. This creates a textured fabric that is reversible, lays flat and looks great alongside other stitches, or even on its own as a standalone pattern.

In the round (over an even number of sts)
Round 1: *K1, p1; repeat from * until end.
Round 2: *K1, p1; repeat from * until end.
Round 3: *P1, k1; repeat from * until end.
Round 4: *P1, k1; repeat from * until end.
Repeat rounds 1–4 for patt.

Worked flat (over an even number of sts)
Row 1 (RS): *K1, p1; repeat from * until end.
Row 2 (WS): *K1, p1; repeat from * until end.
Row 3: *P1, k1; repeat from * until end.
Row 4: *P1, k1; repeat from * until end.
Repeat rows 1–4 for patt.

SHORT ROW SHAPING
German Short Rows

Short rows are a technique used to work extra rows across a portion of the stitches on the needles, lengthening the fabric of a specific area where the short rows are worked. Short rows are commonly used to shape shoulders and lengthen the back piece of a garment, raising the fabric at the back neck. German short rows are a technique used for short row shaping with minimal gaps or distorted stitches.

Step 1: With the right side facing you, work the number of stitches called for in the pattern. Turn work.

Step 2: With the yarn in front, slip the first stitch purlwise. Tug the yarn up and over the needle. This makes a "double" stitch (MDS). Continue working the row as instructed in pattern. Turn work.

Step 3: Slip the next stitch purlwise with the yarn in front. Tug the yarn up and over the needle. This makes another double stitch (MDS). Continue row as instructed in pattern.

Continue following the pattern as instructed. Once you knit your final row, you will resolve these double stitches (DS) by knitting the double stitches together.

Resources

The following list includes many useful links that every knitter or designer should have bookmarked. For example, the Craft Yarn Council has entire sections of their website dedicated to standards and guidelines related to yarn weight, garment measurements, tool sizes and more. The list also includes other popular resources you can use to improve your techniques, browse for yarn or find me on the web.

Craft Yarn Council: www.craftyarncouncil.com

Ravelry: www.ravelry.com

Techniques: Vogue® Knitting, *The Ultimate Knitting Book*

YarnSub: www.yarnsub.com

My website: www.knitwearbyjoan.com

Knitwear by Joan Patterns (Ravelry):
www.ravelry.com/designers/joan-ho

Knitwear by Joan Patterns (Etsy):
www.etsy.com/shop/knitwearbyjoan

About the Author

Joan Ho is an independent knitwear designer specializing in garments and accessories. She is the former co-owner of HANK & HOOK, an online yarn store that brought popular European yarn brands and DIY kits to a North American audience. During this time, she delved into pattern writing and fell in love with the creative aspect of design. She has since published knitting patterns both independently and as a freelance designer.

Joan lives in Mississauga, Ontario, with her husband, Jacky, and their two cats, Tiger and Linden. When not knitting, she's probably busy making something else to wear or for the home. She is equally passionate about theater, cinema and watching live sports. *Cable Knit Style* is her first book.

Her website is knitwearbyjoan.com.

Acknowledgments

TO JACKY
My husband, best friend, and now we can add another title: photographer. Triple threat! Among many other things, thank you for planning this photography trip with me. Thank you for allowing me to steal your carry-on for my knits during the worldwide luggage crisis, for carrying 10 pounds of camera gear on all our hikes, for driving around finding a place for me to charge said camera when I inevitably drained the battery . . . I could go on, but you know I'm forever grateful.

TO MY FAMILY
Mom and Dad, thank you for all your hard work and sacrifice all these years. You showed me early on in life that the arts are worth pursuing and I've taken that to heart ever since. Also, thank you for instilling in me a love for books as a child. Dad, it's so wonderful how this has all come full circle with you having worked in publishing decades ago, and your daughter becoming a published author years later. Jocelyn and Joey, thank you for tolerating my weirdness and giving me the courage to dream big.

TO MY FRIENDS
You know who you are. Thank you for being my biggest fans even during the times when it was difficult to believe in myself. Christie, you have no idea what your support means to me! You're always so quick and helpful with your advice. I'm appreciative of your honest and thoughtful opinions, and I take all your suggestions to heart. Your enthusiasm is infectious, and I carried your support with me throughout this whole process. Loretta, you've been there since day one. You have a way of looking on the bright side of everything, and your words bring so much joy and comfort to my life! I'll always look back fondly at the time we spent together in sewing class. Anna, you're the first person who told me I could write my own knitting patterns. Before that, the idea had never crossed my mind, and I thank you for your encouragement and your steadfast belief in me. I'll always cherish the time we spent building HANK & HOOK from the ground up. I truly believe that without that experience, I would not have been able to pursue this journey.

TO SARA
Thank you so much for all the hard work you've put into making this book happen! Your attention to detail helped elevate my work and gave it a level of finesse that I could not have achieved on my own.

TO PAGE STREET PUBLISHING
Thank you so much for making my childhood dream come true. Never in my wildest dreams would I have imagined even a year ago that this would be a possibility. Thank you for believing in me and giving me the creative freedom to write a book that is a true reflection of my personal style.

TO MY TESTERS
Whether this is the first or fifth time you've tested for me, a million thanks. Please know that your hard work is always appreciated!

TO THE SUPPLIERS
Thank you to the following companies for sending me their beautiful yarns to create the designs in this book. Your generosity is greatly appreciated!

Estelle Yarns
www.estelleyarns.com

Knitting for Olive
www.knittingforolive.com

Nordic Yarn Imports
www.nordicyarnimports.com

Stitch & Story

Wool and the Gang
www.woolandthegang.com

Index

Note: the notations (AB), (I), and (A) following a project name indicate the level of knitting skills needed, as explained on page 8.